THE ZERO INDEX

A Path to Sustainable Safety Excellence

THE **ZERO INDEX**

Zero Index and Safety in Action are trademarks of
Behavioral Science Technology, Inc.

Published by Behavioral Science Technology, Inc., Ojai, California.

ISBN: 978-0-9667569-0-6

Printed in the United States of America.

10 9 8 7 6 5 4 3 2 1

Cover image iStockphoto.com/©Pavel Klyuykov
Book Design & Layout, Cover Design: Julie Knudsen

THE ZERO INDEX

INDEX

A Path to Sustainable
Safety Excellence

Colin Duncan, General Editor

Rebecca Nigel, Editor

Foreword by Thomas R. Krause, Ph.D.

SAFETY IN
ACTION
PRESS
An imprint of BST

TABLE OF CONTENTS

THE ZERO
INDEX

FOREWORD

The concept of "maturity" has been around for many years in the safety community and it has been useful, especially when it was first introduced 20 years ago or so.

The idea that organizations go through stages in the development of their capability to provide safety excellence to their employees has been of benefit —to communications, to understanding barriers, and for planning improvements. Organizations in the early stages of the development of safety capability have different sets of issues than those faced in later stages, and so need different strategies.

We at BST have long felt that the next step forward in the area of safety maturity was to move from a one-dimensional scale, which tends to paint development in broad and over-generalized strokes, to a set of scales that represent the full complement of factors that contribute to the development of safety excellence. Getting to zero injuries and fatalities requires nothing less.

This book is an outline of those factors, assembled from years of consulting engagements and thousands of data sets. It lays out the set of disciplines we have found to be most important to safety excellence and describes a series of anchor points that mark the maturity of each discipline as it is developed. This granularity enables the organization to identify itself and to self-assess where it is along the continuum of maturity for each discipline. An organization can take stock of the things it has accomplished to get to that point—and identify the things needed to get to the next level.

We have also included a chapter on our latest research on serious injuries and fatalities. No organization can claim it is fully mature in the safety arena if it continues to have serious injuries and fatalities. Addressing this critically important area is both a fulfillment of maturity and a mechanism for improvement at the same time.

We welcome your comments and wish you good reading as you come to grips with the Zero Index.

Thomas R. Krause, Ph.D.
Founder and Senior Advisor on
Research and Thought Leadership,
BST

ACKNOWLEDGEMENTS

This book was made possible through the collaboration of an outstanding group of   people. Each of the contributing authors is an expert in his or her own right and this book would not exist without their work both inside these pages and in the field. The Zero Index was no less shaped by our client organizations whose dedication to the wellbeing of their employees, contractors, and communities continually inspires us to advance the way we understand and support safety performance improvement. Special thanks go to BNSF for being among the early adopters of the assessment process using the Zero Index model and for giving us feedback that fueled further refinement in our thinking.

There are many colleagues at BST whose work, in ways direct and indirect, have helped shape the development of the principles outlined in this book. Kristen Bell's work analyzing client data laid the foundation for the disciplines of the Zero Index framework. In addition, Scott Stricoff led the development of real-world applications of the Zero Index. He has been assisted in this work by Jim Huggett, Mike Mangan, Ricky Yu, Tom Graham, Henri Chan, Pearlyn Lim, and Richard Russell.

Finally, putting ideas into print requires the successful collaboration of the book's authors with a number of experts and advisors. We are grateful to Alison Black for her research expertise and to Seb Blair and Rick Smith for insights into their client work. Maija Rothenberg provided her editorial guidance and Dave Johnson his perspective as a safety journalist. Julie Knudsen's thoughtful design of the cover, graphics, and layout greatly enhanced the accessibility of the material. And I would be remiss not to mention Rebecca Nigel for her management of the project, her outstanding writing and editing skills, and for helping the authors speak with one voice.

Our heartfelt thanks go to everyone who contributed to the book's success.

Colin Duncan, General Editor
CEO of BST

INTRODUCTION
Colin Duncan

The purpose of this book is to change the way you think about safety—to help you understand where you are today and where you need to be in the future. Drawn from the best thinking of practitioners in the field, and our research over many years, this book presents all we have learned to date from our clients around the world. It is designed to be a practical, accessible tool for identifying clear actions for improvement. We hope it will be the sort of book in which you will be able to scribble notes in the margins and at the end of each chapter, to refer back to as you navigate toward your ultimate goal: 100% safe, at all times, for your employees and anyone who interacts with your operations and your products.

Our work over the past 30 years has shown us that some organizations are distinctly different in how they think and act with respect to safety. They tend to focus on inputs rather than outputs. They excel at engaging employees and creating a compelling vision of what safety is and could be. They are rigorous and proactive in their use of safety systems and safety measures, and have progressive decision-making structures that take risk into account far ahead of imminent danger.

In other words, they practice discernible disciplines that can be assessed, learned, and improved.

THE NEED TO MOVE FORWARD

In 1988, an explosion and fire aboard the North Sea rig Piper Alpha left 167 men dead, nearly £2 billion (US $3.4 billion) in damage and lost production, and a local community and its families devastated by the loss. At the time, the CEO of Occidental Petroleum infamously remarked, "We have done all we can to prevent catastrophic failures like this one."

In 2010, history seemed to repeat itself on the Deepwater Horizon platform. This time the loss of control of a wellhead led to an explosion and fire that killed 11 workers. What followed was a public relations nightmare as the media played out a narrative of technical and management failure against a backdrop of environmental disaster. The persistent question was, *Why? Haven't we advanced safety engineering and practice over these past 20 years? Haven't we learned from the past?* Like his predecessor before him, BP's then CEO was at a loss to explain it, saying simply, "Sometimes you step off the curb and get hit by a bus." What his statement suggests is that despite an evolution in engineering and technical ability that has allowed industry to realize incredible achievement, our understanding of risk, specifically its identification and mitigation, has lagged woefully behind.

Now as then, the apparent resignation, and sometimes outright fatalism, surrounding safety in modern industry is notably incongruous with the organizational and technological advancement of the past 25 years. Few leaders today would consider explaining poor production, low quality, or operating losses as "bad luck". Yet we still hear some accept safety failures as just that. We know from our work with organizations around the world that senior leaders care deeply about the wellbeing of their people. We know that given the right information, they are capable of moving their organizations forward in remarkable ways. Yet, consistent and coherent safety performance continues to elude many organizations.

The truth is that safety performance is not a function of luck, chance, or circumstance. Consider the fact that over the last 10 years we have seen non-fatal injury rates drop by 25% or 50% or more in many regions. There are notable success stories, such as the South African mining industry's significant reduction in fatalities over the last five years (we discuss the complexity of serious and fatal injury prevention in chapter 10). Anecdotally, from our work with organizations in the field, we have seen many organizations go months, if not years, without a lost-time or life-altering injury. Many organizations make substantial improvements in injury rates through a rigorous and disciplined approach to understanding risk and taking action on those risks.

The question is not whether safety excellence is possible, but what makes it possible.

SAFETY AS STRATEGY

Achieving a truly zero-harm organization starts with taking a huge step back from our existing ideas and assumptions. This book introduces a state of functioning that we call Zero Index performance: the sustained practice of mitigating exposure to anyone who interacts with an organization and its activities and products—not just your employees but also your customers, vendors, visitors, and community.

Safety performance can be roughly grouped into low, average, and high levels that denote the sophistication and fluency with which the organization applies key disciplines. To create the model we call the Zero Index, we've created a dynamic scale that starts at the low end of safety performance with Avoidance-driven, continues in the middle with Compliance-driven, and ends with Values-driven—the state of zero harm (Figure 0-1).

Figure 0-1

At the Avoidance level of safety performance, safety is a burdensome necessity. At the Compliance level, it is a priority, an important goal. But at the Values level, safety is not just a value for the organization—it is who we are.

Zero Index organizations are distinguished by their ability to take a big picture view of safety performance. In Zero Index, safety is not a program but an integral business function that is influenced by—and, in turn, influences—operational execution. Zero Index performance is characteristically:

- **Comprehensive:** Safety activities are guided by a detailed, granular strategy developed from a comprehensive understanding of the gap between where the organization is and where it desires to be. The organization acts on a holistic picture of safety performance; the goal is bigger than any single area or outcome.

- **Anticipatory:** Safety performance is driven by a sophisticated set of metrics that detect changes in exposure before such changes create events.

- **Externally and internally focused:** The organization adapts to changes that influence exposure within and outside the organization.

- **Integrated:** Safety activities are coordinated across functions; they complement other business systems and processes and show a high degree of skill and sophistication. The organization executes safety in concert with other business goals; the line between "work" and "safety" has disappeared, because real work is expected to be safe work, and the activities that make work safe are a regular part of the work, not something accomplished separately by a separate team.

- **Risk based versus outcome based:** Exposure is the measure of progress (Is exposure going down? Do we know where the exposures are?) and the trigger for change (we act when exposure changes, not just when exposure leads to actual injury).

In a Zero Index organization, safety performance is no longer treated as something "other"; the goals, activities, planning, and results are a natural part of the organization's overall performance, integrated with day-to-day business functions and decisions. Safety is not thought to be in opposition to business goals, the way it is sometimes looked on as an important (but separate) consideration during, say, the design of a new piece of equipment.

Clearly, achieving this level of performance is not easy. No organization starts out as a Zero Index organization. In safety, as with all human endeavors, excellence is achieved in stages.

In Section I, *Safety at a Crossroads,* we will discuss the development of safety performance over the past three decades, which has seen organizations move from a limited technical and tactical focus to the wiser recognition that leadership, culture, and behavior have to support the entirety of the organizational system as it relates to safety—not just one part of the system.

In Section II, *The Art of What's Possible,* we describe what the Zero Index is. We ask a number of questions: What does a zero-harm organization look like? What are its components? How would you describe zero-harm performance in terms that you could observe, measure—and, most important—move toward? We will explain the 10 practices, or disciplines, that make up the Zero Index model.

In Section III, *Creating the Zero Index Organization,* we describe how to get there from here—how to bridge the gap between fundamental (Compliance-driven) safety performance and the more advanced (Values-driven) mindset of "Safety is who we are." We provide the tools to help you assess your current stage of safety functioning and determine your intervention plan. Making safety a strategic objective is, at its core, a change-management process. We discuss how to remove barriers to change so that you can execute for long-term improvement, making optimum use of available resources.

This is a book for CEOs, COOs, executives, leaders, and professionals on how to build a world-class organization and meet and exceed the needs of all stakeholders. One could argue that the fact that we're talking about a particular aspect of performance—safety—is incidental: the principles discussed in this book can be applied more broadly. But safety is an ideal place to begin organizational change, because it is one of the most fundamental drives of human beings. Safety is bedrock. If you can do safety well, you can do other things well.

Our ultimate aim is to help you as a CEO, COO, executive, plant manager, or safety leader understand the gap between where you are and where you want to be—so you can manage toward a future goal while avoiding the trap of programs and fads. We hope this book helps you get there.

NOTES

PART I:

Safety at a Crossroads

THE QUIET CRISIS

by R. Scott Stricoff

THE QUIET CRISIS

Imagine an organization in which everyone is safe, all the time.

Imagine a workplace where people's investment in safety transcends organizational boundaries, where—regardless of level or function—safety is never "your" job or "their" job, it is *our* job. Here, leaders know the risks most likely to lead to accidents and can describe in detail what they are doing to address the issues. Incidents are so infrequent that analyzing them after the fact is almost meaningless. Instead of just looking backward, responding to what has already happened, senior leaders and safety professionals pore over indicative data each month to find where the "next one" could happen.

Imagine an organization where the commitment to safety as a value is as unshakable and unmovable as a mountain in a rainstorm. It is a place where:

- Performance isn't judged on outcome alone but on all the factors that influence safety functioning, with the explicit goal of protecting the well-being of every person who interacts with the organization.

- Safety systems anticipate and prepare for future risks, and these systems are aligned with, and supported by, other business processes and decisions.

- Senior executives understand the multiple influences on exposures and partner with safety professionals, division leaders, and site leaders in reducing them.

- The safety professional is not an isolated technical expert, but an esteemed partner in organizational change.

- Employees at all levels take on safety leadership roles and are encouraged and supported to fill them.

- Outside forces may put pressure on the organization to take shortcuts or skip processes to achieve higher profitability, but it stands firm, putting the safety of everyone first.

Is such an organization possible?

We believe it is. In fact, we see glimpses of it continually. We see hints in organizations that extend exposure reduction practices to contractors and customers, and in companies that pay out safety bonuses for efforts to reduce risk, even if profitability targets haven't been met. We see it when leaders partner with safety professionals in executing organizational change and when engineers consult front-line employees when designing new systems, processes, and facilities. In the thousands of organizations with whom we have partnered over the years, we have seen shining examples of enlightened safety leadership that transcend limited definitions of safety success as a focus on injury rates alone.

Few organizations, however, achieve this level of performance consistently or comprehensively. More often than not, excellence is concentrated in a handful of areas. For example, in a major oil company you might see a strong focus on safety in downstream production but a weaker focus in upstream operations. Achieving consistency across all the factors that contribute to safety excellence proves much more difficult.

The dilemma is reminiscent of a story about an accomplished singer who was once asked how she was able to sing so beautifully. "It's not hard to sing a beautiful note," she replied. "What's hard is to make every note sound beautiful." In other words, high performance is more than a singular instance of excellence; it is created through successive moments strung together into a harmonious whole. In music, a song cannot have just one or two beautiful notes; all the notes must be sung well, with the right expression, in harmony with others. They must be arranged in the right key, in the right order, to create a pleasing pattern. In safety, organizations create high performance through executing multiple disciplines in concert, with everyone singing from the same score.

What do you imagine for your organization?

THE NEXT EVOLUTION

The development of safety performance over the past 20 years has seen leading organizations move from a technical and tactical focus to the recognition that leadership, culture, and behavior have to support the entire system that drives safety outcomes. Safety outcomes around the world and throughout industry have improved significantly. For instance, between 1998 and 2008 nonfatal injuries in the United States have declined by 45%.[1] In Germany, reported injuries dropped by 33%; in the United Kingdom, 25%; in Sweden, 30%.[2]

---

1   U.S. Bureau of Labor Statistics. Data available at www.bls.gov.

2   International Labor Organization, *LABORSTA Labor Statistics Database, 1998–2010* (Geneva). Available at www.ilo.org.

Despite these advances, safety continues to be dominated by a project-engineering mindset. Organizational goals of "zero harm" are approached through a succession of discrete activities that rarely form a comprehensive strategy. Innovation is often driven in fits and starts by whatever fads are currently in favor. Organizations, even those considered to be high performers in safety, commonly implement programs without defining a coherent vision of how all the parts fit together. It is not uncommon to

Many leaders want to create an organization in which "zero harm" is a reality, yet few can describe what that means.

find that existing systems are overlooked as new ones are added—or worse, multiple layers are built on top of what already exists, like old layers of a forgotten civilization buried deep beneath the city streets. This gives the overall safety management framework a shaky foundation, a system that is too complex to understand and too cumbersome to manage.

In the simplest terms, safety is suffering a crisis of execution. Safety is simultaneously touted as an essential part of organizational life while being managed as an abstraction separate from daily organizational realities. Employees know that safety is important, yet they continue to run into obstacles to safe work in the so-called non-safety systems and processes (we would argue that all systems are safety related). We know the elements that reduce exposure, yet we have difficulty creating an overarching framework that collectively supports them.

Our work with organizations in more than 70 countries suggests that the next evolution in safety will be a cohesive strategic focus combined with a more disciplined execution. Many innovations in the field (such as employee engagement mechanisms and process safety standards) have already provided excellent systems, advanced our understanding of various elements (such as the connection between culture and safety outcomes), and better oriented people at all levels to their roles and responsibilities. The sea change in safety will not be adding to these so much as pulling them together to create a cohesive approach to safety performance. Fundamentally, the new focus will be on learning how to develop and execute safety strategy at the operational level and on integrating safety with the strategic functioning of the business as a whole. Moreover, it will be about helping personnel at every level connect themselves to the execution of safety and to the creation of a high-performance culture—that is, the development of a shared assumption about how things are done and what is valued.

How will we get there? Achieving the ultimate goal of everyone safe, all the time, requires a new framework to unify the existing, disparate parts. It requires new ideas about what safety is—and what safety could be.

Our foundation for these new ideas draws on four premises:

1. **Safety requires strategic oversight.** Comprehensive execution requires the coordination of multiple disciplines and contributors. Executives, safety professionals, operational leaders, and others must understand all the constituent parts of safety (the foundational, safety, and organizational disciplines—to be discussed in part two) and how to manage them under a cohesive system. The future state we develop must allow organizations to focus on both short-term priorities and long-term objectives and ensure appropriate balance in the formulation and execution of the change that is required. Safety commands strategic standing in organizations that have come to understand the fundamental link between workplace safety and organizational excellence, not to mention the underlying ethic of doing the right thing.

2. **Safety is imperative to sustainability.** The safety goal is inseparable from the well-being of the organization. The ability to deliver on the promise of zero harm to employees, contractors, customers, and community is foundational to the ability to deliver excellence in other objectives. The next generation of safety performance requires developing an understanding of safety's presence, influence, and importance in all aspects of operational life.

3. **Safety is a platform.** Consistently reducing risk requires ongoing attention to the systems, leadership, and culture that support operational functioning. The future of safety excellence will demand an articulation of the links between safety and the organization, and between safety and other performance goals, so that safety becomes woven into the fabric of the organization rather than remaining on the sidelines, functionally discrete.

4. **Safety is systemic.** Change will take more than a program; it will take an approach based on sound change execution principles and a sophisticated understanding of organizational functioning. Safety outcomes are immediately created wherever the "work" gets done, be it the shop floor, the coal face, the platform, or the field. But the circumstances, conditions, decisions, and practices that lead to these outcomes often begin much further upstream. Exposure to injury is just as often created—or mitigated by—the intersection of people and systems in the board room or the production office as it is at the front line. Becoming an organization in which "Safety is who we are" requires changing the whole system that influences the exposure, not just the immediate pathway.

HOW WE GOT WHERE WE ARE TODAY

We live in a time when worker health and safety are better than at any time in history. Workers in the industrialized world generally enjoy greater benefits, and work fewer hours, than in previous generations. Advances in technology, regulatory oversight, business practices, and societal expectations have created a landscape in which an industrial job is no longer a sure sentence to a short, hard life. Yet for all these advances, the performance of safety efforts across industry reveals a discipline that is stuck in neutral. The pace of overall injury reductions is slower now than it was a generation ago, while the rate of fatal and serious events has remained effectively flat. Advancements in our understanding of leadership and culture, while critical, are often superficially applied with equally superficial results. In many organizations, safety performance is made up of a series of fragmented activities that never connect to a greater whole or to the core of the organization itself.

Fundamentally, the problem is that safety performance has failed to mature into an integrated organizational discipline. While there have been many advances to pieces of the safety picture, the practice as a whole is still strongly influenced by the forces and events that helped to shape it. So in order to define the future of safety, we will first examine its past.

Four Decades of Industrial Safety Practice

The passage of the U.S. Occupational Safety and Health Act (OSH Act) in 1970 marked the beginning of the modern era of industrial safety in the United States, and ultimately across the globe. While some countries had begun addressing workplace safety and health earlier (e.g., Brazil in 1968; Malaysia in 1969), the formalized action on the OSH Act in the U.S. helped focus attention on workplace health and safety and was followed by similar legislation in many other countries, such as the U.K.'s Health and Safety at Work Act (1974), and laws at the state and provincial level in Canada and Australia. Prior to the 1970s the regulatory environment in the U.S. was highly varied. Some states had active programs dating back to World War II, while others were more laissez-faire. Some large companies were active in protecting worker health and safety, while others were not.

In the initial years of the modern safety era the primary focus was on establishing a baseline of regulation by adopting existing industry consensus standards as formal regulations while establishing new inspection capabilities to enforce these rules. Many of these new regulations tended to include detailed specifications, and much of the enforcement action that resulted was focused on detailed facility characteristics (such as the apocryphal citations for guard rail height being off by one inch). By and large, the focus of industry during the 1970s, after the passage of OSH Act, was on bringing facilities into conformance with government specifications—on the letter of the law, in other words, rather than the spirit.

From this phase of activity, industry moved to a focus on compliance assurance—implementing audit programs to try to prevent citations. Generally, this activity was not a risk-based effort to reduce exposure to hazards but rather was designed to assure executives and boards that organizations were in compliance with government rules. Although the audit programs provided some feel-good comfort that the government's minimum standards of performance were being met, they did little to drive continuous risk reduction or improve safety results.

This audit focus evolved into a focus on management systems—how the organization could implement management processes that would ensure compliance rather than simply auditing to find deviations. This tended to coincide with the general interest in Total Quality Management (TQM) thinking, introduced in the 1980s, and the widespread understanding that it was better to build quality into the process from the get-go rather than simply inspect for it at the end of the process. However, a lack of discernment about which systems were really important led in some cases to a bureaucratic preponderance of systems and procedures that did little to truly influence safety.

Along with interest in TQM came a growing acceptance of behavior-based safety as a tool for safety performance improvement. As the third leg of the stool (complementing the other two legs of facility improvements and management systems), effective behavior-based safety systems harnessed the engagement of employees in identifying barriers to safe behavior and reinforcing safe behavior. Unfortunately, the growing popularity of behavior-based safety led to the "behavior-based safety" label being applied inaccurately to all sorts of approaches, ranging from incentive programs to supervisory "gotcha" inspections, leaving many people confused about what the real behavior-based safety approach entailed.

What has been the evolution of safety in your organization and industry?

The Bhopal tragedy of 1984,[3] the worst industrial accident in history, during which thousands of people lost their lives, brought widespread attention to an entirely different aspect of industrial safety—the risk of catastrophic accidents with the potential to cause massive numbers of injuries and fatalities.

---

3   See, for example: Edward Broughton, "The Bhopal Disaster and Its Aftermath," *Environmental Health*, 4 (1): 6 pages.

More specifically, the events in Bhopal led to the development of a field called "process safety," something distinct from "personal safety." Process safety was initially limited to the chemical industry, but was sometimes adopted beyond that field. In the wake of Bhopal, there were extensive efforts by industry associations (such as the American Chemistry Council—then known as the Chemical Manufacturers Association), professional associations (such as the American Institute of Chemical Engineers), and government agencies as well as individual companies to better address process safety risk. This led to the publication of guidelines, the establishment of industry programs, and ultimately the adoption of government regulations. The regulations were noteworthy in that they represented the first broad set of rules that required interrelated management systems to understand and manage a category of risk (rather than simply specifying control measures.)

In the last decade we have seen growing attention paid to the impact of culture and leadership on safety. Detailed examinations of serious incidents, such as the disasters at Sasol's Secunda Refinery and BHP's Moura Mine and the accident with NASA's Columbia space shuttle, have highlighted organizational culture as an important contributing factor to the incidents. The importance of culture and leadership has held true during examinations of many of the smaller and less serious incidents and near misses that occur regularly in industry.

SOME PROGRESS, BUT NOT ENOUGH

If we look back at where we were 40 years ago, we see significant progress. In the U.S., the overall workplace injury rate and the rate for lost time injuries have both shown major declines. Looking more closely, however, we see that the rate of workplace fatalities has been essentially level for close to 10 years, and the rate of injuries involving days away from work has shown little decline in this period.[4] Available injury and fatality data from Europe show the same recent trend. This raises the questions:

- Where do we go from here?

- How do we move ever closer to the goal of every worker returning home every day in the same condition in which he or she started the day?

- How do we weave safety into the fabric and functioning of the organization the way we have with finance, quality, and other disciplines?

4   *New Findings on Serious Injuries and Fatalities*, 2011, (Ojai, California). Viewed at www.bstsolutions.com.

In the various paths toward improvement since 1970, safety has had an evolving but always limited focus. Safety is driven by narrow trends. But in the absence of a more comprehensive picture of what it takes to achieve truly sustainable, outstanding safety performance, these trends are often introduced in a vacuum, without real alignment or connection to the fundamental forces driving the way organizations work. It's common for organizations to introduce safety management mechanisms that are inconsistent with the priorities and consequences established by performance management systems—for example, rewarding productivity and "up time" while expecting supervisors to enforce safety procedures that are perceived to cause delays and to have no apparent benefit. We have tried to train people into safe behavior without understanding why workers appear to take risks. We have attempted to consider how culture influences safety systems without understanding that this is a two-way street—that the systems, and not just the safety systems, also influence the culture.

The result has been a fragmented understanding of safety excellence and what it takes to get there. As a result, workers see safety initiatives as lacking seriousness and commitment, executives are frustrated over their inability to achieve goals, and the layers in the middle are overburdened by a growing collection of initiatives, programs, slogans, and ideas that are never optimized or streamlined.

To understand where to go from here, we need to look at several key issues: the influence of regulations, the role of indicators, and the lack of clarity about who has safety expertise.

Regulatory Influence

Government and regulators play a role in influencing the direction of safety efforts. Much attention is paid by the public and the media to regulatory enforcement activities, which, by their very nature, strive for a least common denominator of performance. Through a ponderous process, regulations are established that reflect the compromises made to accommodate the interests of a great many constituent parties, compromises that have the effect of establishing a minimum standard of acceptable performance that tends to lag the state of the art of our understanding by many years. Although enforcement of such regulations is necessary to address the segments of industry that would do little without being forced, a great many industrial organizations, especially within the most hazardous industries, are far ahead of regulatory requirements.

However, the impact of government on safety and health extends beyond regulation, in ways that are far more subtle. One significant example is in the way governments mandate that workers be compensated for injuries and illnesses suffered on the job. The workers compensation system that applies to most manufacturing in the U.S. is a no-fault system in which workers are ensured prompt compensation while employers are provided with economic limits on

Case management has become a major area of effort, with people sometimes mistaking this for a safety activity.

the cost of injury. These systems have established rules to govern compensability and those rules influence the way people report injuries and manage their outcomes. Where workers compensation does not apply, we see the impact of alternative approaches. In the railroad industry, compensation for injuries is governed by the Federal Employers Liability Act, or FELA, a fault-based system. Where FELA applies, we see a huge focus on fault finding and blame that drives the behavior of management and workers alike in their reactions to injuries and near misses. What is needed, and what neither fault finding nor blame provides, is a system that emphasizes a focus on understanding how to better prevent injuries.

Case management has become a major area of effort, with people sometimes mistaking this for a safety activity. Case management focuses on the efficiency and effectiveness of treatment following an injury, which can have major impacts on costs, injury classification (lost time versus non-lost time),

As a safety leader, what is your biggest concern now?

and returning people to work more rapidly. However, case management is a retrospective activity—it does not attempt to identify exposures or prevent injuries. The very best case management systems in the world will not lead to an injury-free workplace.

The Role of Indicators

One of the most important contributions of the U.S. Occupational Safety and Health Act was the establishment of a uniform system of safety statistics administered by the Bureau of Labor Statistics (BLS). The injury rates recorded by employers and reported by BLS are often criticized, with good reason. The attention placed on injury rates in many organizations creates pressure to focus on injury classification rather than on injury prevention, and the ambiguity inherent in the OSHA/BLS (and arguably any) system of injury classification has led to embarrassing compliance problems, in some cases even at companies that are known for their serious approach to safety. Despite the faults of this system, having a single, consistent metric for safety outcomes has been valuable, because it provides a basis for evaluating trends and motivating improvement.

That said, the absence of a more robust scorecard of safety metrics in many organizations creates a serious gap in efforts to manage safety. Measuring injury rates alone with no meaningful leading indicators is like trying to manage a business when the only information available is the profit figure after each quarter ends. In early April we would find out whether we made money in the first quarter of the year, but we would not know why. We may have had improved revenue, or reduced material costs, or improved productivity, or fewer product returns, but all we would know is that we made money and we hoped it would continue. The next steps that organizations should be taking are to (1) understand which metrics are true leading indicators of performance for their organizations, (2) adopt these metrics as key performance indicators, and (3) integrate them with performance management.

All too often we have assumed that individual worker motivation was the key to reducing injuries. Gimmicks, giveaways, bonuses, and retraining have been fallback elements commonly used in response to pressure for injury rate improvement. This thinking has tended to underestimate, and in some cases ignore, the powerful impact of the entire context of work on safety performance. It also plays to the ridiculous notion that getting hurt is avoided by perks. Safety does not happen in a vacuum. Individual workers and their supervisors and managers function in an environment in which there are a wide variety of demands imposed by both the workplace and the personal lives people lead outside of the workplace. When we identify exposure to safety hazards, whether it occurs following an injury or through anticipatory hazard assessment activity, it is critical that identification of the causes and approaches to prevention include really thorough consideration of all factors that have created the risk.

Who's the Safety Leader?

We find ourselves in an environment in which the role of safety practitioner is confused. Some individuals who have specialized safety responsibility are engineers and other technical professionals (e.g., industrial hygienists), some others are trainers, and still others come from manufacturing backgrounds and have been diverted into safety specialist roles. Few organizations have found effective ways to fully align the role of a safety specialist with the widely accepted concept that responsibility for safety performance must rest with line management. Some safety specialists are essentially auditors, some write rules for others to implement, and still others are advisors whose roles become very passive. It is the rare excep-

The senior-most safety leader should be a high-potential employee—a future CEO.

tion to see someone with broad and deep safety experience and knowledge who has developed the skills and achieved the organizational position to function as an effective organizational change agent—someone who can actually influence the organization's functioning at fundamental levels. In many cases, unfortunately, being a safety practitioner is seen as a "retirement" job.

LOOKING BACK TO LOOK FORWARD

The journey in pursuit of safety excellence in the last four decades has been akin to traveling through a dense forest without a map. Time and again, we as an industry took the first path we came across. Initially, the priorities for modern safety efforts were largely determined by the happenstance of existing consensus standards that could be adopted to jump-start fledgling regulatory agencies. While those standards presumably existed because they addressed issues that were of concern, their development had occurred piecemeal, without any overall plan or strategy. As we moved on from those initial standards we came upon various forks in the road—again, based on happenstance, e.g., the focus on PSM driven by the disaster in Bhopal, and the focus on culture driven by the Columbia and Texas City incidents.

To achieve the ultimate objective of sustainable excellence in safety—of a discipline integrated into the fabric and functioning of the organization—we need a more cohesive and coherent vision and plan. Organizations need a better understanding of the direction in which they need to head and how to get there, taking into considering the characteristics of, and challenges faced by, their individual situations. Although we may have lacked a roadmap up to this point, we have the opportunity to jump ahead in our understanding —to create, in essence, a GPS device that can reveal both a clear destination and the steps we must navigate to get there.

NOTES

NOTES

SAFETY'S COMMON FRAMEWORK

by Donald R. Groover and Richard Russell

SAFETY'S COMMON FRAMEWORK

To the outside observer, one of the most striking things about workplace safety is the variety of its practices and types. If you were to ask a dozen people what safety is, you would likely hear a dozen different answers. For some, safety is about the prevention of occupational injuries. For others, it is the prevention of catastrophic events such as the Texas City chemical explosion of 1947, the Bhopal gas tragedy of 1984, or the Deepwater Horizon explosion and oil spill of 2010. For others still, the word safety brings to mind images of motor vehicle or rail incidents, food product safety, and aircraft disasters—or medical errors and patient safety. The categorization of safety into various types has led to the development of specialties, each with its own experts and standards. Certainly, one could argue for treating each safety specialty as a serious field in its own right. The particulars required to execute rail safety differ considerably from those of food safety, for example, and the safety practices essential to reducing harm to linemen in the utility industry are necessarily distinct from much of the process safety controls used in a chemical operation.

The purpose of this book, however, is not to further break safety down into its disparate parts, but rather to recast the conventional wisdom about what is possible. The purpose is to identify safety's common principles, or rules, and to show how they are manifested as disciplines that organizations in any industry can assess, develop, and improve. Ultimately, safety advancement is about fluency of understanding and practice. Specifically, advancement requires a framework that helps organizations adapt particular systems and practices as the needs of the business and its people change, not the other way around. Just as someone who fully understands the tenets of architecture has a significant advantage over someone who knows only how to read a blueprint, the leader who understands safety's core principles has more tools for improvement than someone who is proficient at the practices of a single industry or discipline. The key to discovering and leveraging these principles is learning how to distinguish the essentials from the particulars.

DIFFERENCES IN SAFETY

Types of safety, like the industries they support, are most often classified by the product or service provided by organizations in that sector: transportation, mining, and manufacturing, for example—or are even further divided within industry, such as nuclear safety within the utility industry. By extension, the nature of the output necessarily creates differences in work processes, environments, and other variables, including safety. Safety practices necessarily differ depending on the unique characteristics of a particular organization or work—e.g., by typical injury causation, injury consequences, and injury frequency. Safety is also shaped by external factors, such as the public attention garnered by accidents in that particular industry, the amount of regulatory oversight, and the availability of safety data.

Let's take a brief look at some of the elements that affect how safety is executed. Within each category, note the distinction between individual workplace injuries and process safety incidents.

Injury Causation

Individual workplace injuries commonly result from the unintended interaction of an individual with equipment, with an energy source, or with a contaminant. When it comes to life altering workplace injuries, they often result from common causal factors such as falls from heights (e.g., from ladders or elevated work stations), working on equipment that is not fully de-energized, or interactions with mobile equipment, to mention a few. Contrast this with process safety incidents, in which catastrophic events usually result from a breakdown in the system, leading to failure of a critical piece of equipment, or with patient safety, in which the most common causes of patient harm are illegible handwriting on prescriptions and a failure to wash hands. These causes appear to be so different that it is natural, though incorrect, to assume they require different approaches to mitigation.

Injury Consequences

For many organizations, workplace injuries caused by factors related to personal safety may have relatively small economic consequences to the employer, even in the case of fatalities and the most serious injuries. The human toll of individual workplace injuries is limited, in the sense that most incidents involve one individual (or, in rare instances, a few individuals). Although the impact on these individuals can be very significant, the number affected is small. Major process safety incidents, product contamination, or airline disasters, on the other hand, can have very large economic consequences in terms of damage to the company's property, lost production, liability for third-party injuries and fatalities, and damage to others' property. The human toll of major process safety incidents is often larger, including multiple fatalities and serious injuries, the effect of which sometimes extends beyond the employee population to the general public. Similarly, whereas medical errors typically affect one person at a time and thus have limited cost in both human and economic terms, a plane crash has the potential to affect hundreds of individuals.

Frequency

In the United States each year, for example, approximately 4% of workers in general manufacturing industries sustain an injury requiring more than first aid treatment, and on average, approximately 12 people die each day from workplace injuries. Individual automobile accidents are an everyday occurrence: nearly 34,000 people die in auto crashes annually in the United States alone. In contrast, major process safety incidents and commercial airplane crashes occur much less frequently. Addressing infrequent versus everyday occurrences would appear to suggest the need for different approaches.

Visibility

Major process safety incidents, product contamination incidents, and nuclear disasters attract widespread public attention, as do injuries to airplane and mass transit passengers. However, it is rare for a workplace injury to receive broad public attention. Auto crashes are considered routine. In part, this is a result of their frequency, but it is also because incidents that affect one or two people at a time do not attract public attention the way a mass casualty incident does. Public attention creates greater pressure for prevention.

Regulatory Requirements and Governance

The way in which safety is addressed by local, regional, and federal governments also differs across sectors. In most countries a government agency is responsible for workplace safety and health standards. However, several government agencies are generally responsible for transportation safety. Whereas workplace safety and transportation are subject to considerable regulation, patient safety is more often than not a matter of self-regulation.

Safety Data

There is widespread disparity regarding the availability of data (incidents and near misses) related to safety in the various sectors. Many countries have comprehensive rules for reporting workplace injury data, but near-miss data are left up to individual companies, and few collect it in meaningful ways. In most countries, air transportation has a close-call reporting system and a data-compilation system for incidents (including incidents that consist of procedural violations that have no actual adverse impact), both of which provide further insight into causation. On the other hand, process safety and patient safety have no consolidated reporting system, making it very difficult to understand the magnitude of the issues or to perform the analyses that could support improvement efforts.

THE CASE FOR A COMMON FRAMEWORK

Given the seemingly vast differences in practice and thinking, how do we even start to develop a common framework for safety?

We start at the beginning.

Understanding what makes safety different—and the same—is the start of a common framework. All safety "types" share a common foundation. Fundamentally, organizational safety anywhere is aimed at reducing or eliminating exposure to harm. All types of safety must contend with the same laws of physics and with human and organizational dynamics. While their safety systems are radically different, if they are effective, railroads, airlines, steel mills, hospitals, food manufacturers, and chemical plants execute safety based on the same core set of rules. Safety principles such as the hierarchy of controls,[1] is applicable whether you are pouring molten metal or producing coffee products. Similarly, there are cultural tenets, such as reciprocity and perceived organizational support, that shape the work practices and openness to change essential to safety functioning in any organization. Many experienced leaders and safety professionals already understand these rules implicitly. Yet the persistent and sometimes absolute distinction of safety by industry, exposure, activity, and so on, have made the development of a common framework—and the common learnings that come with it—nearly impossible. Distinctions are essential. The problem is learning how to make them the right way.

Making the Right Distinctions: Culture vs. Culture

An example of the kind of distinction safety leaders need to make can be found in the experience of many companies grappling with managing global operations. A popular myth suggests that regional or national culture determines safety performance. In some organizations, poor results are expected in certain regions (e.g., developing nations). Leaders may say things such as, "People there just don't value life the way 'we' do," or "Workers in that region aren't very educated." This belief is a way of explaining away real variances and making high injury and fatality rates "acceptable" by tying them to perceived differences in people.

If that idea were true, we should be able to predict injury rates simply by a worksite's location or by the so-called type of people working there. And yet we see significant variation all the time, even when weighted for industry, em-

---

1   The hierarchy of controls is a principle that defines a tiered progression of risk mitigation, from more through less effective types, given a particular task. Typically, a hierarchy may start with elimination of the hazard (most preferred) and progress to personal protective equipment/PPE (least preferred).

ployee population, and work processes. There are many examples of global organizations where safety performance is better in developing nations than developed nations. Incorrect assumptions (too often passed along without question) about regional culture and safety actually arise from a failure to distinguish between types of culture. Without question, there are significant contrasts and challenges among national and regional cultures that do have implications in the workplace. For example, in some places there is great resistance to communicating upwards to a superior, while in other places people revel in the opportunity to do so, to the point of questioning every instruction. In some parts of the world just getting basic safety equipment can be a challenge and in some instances leadership may not be educated about safety rules and regulations nor fluent in their ability to successfully lead safety. Comparing metrics across regions adds to the confusion; high variation in the quality and reliability of injury data suggests (to some leaders) that the data are representative of the local culture, or that they predetermine future success (or lack thereof).

The reality is that organizations operate within layers of different types of culture: national, regional, local—even subcultures within the same location. The type of culture that matters immediately to safety outcomes is organizational culture, the "how we do things here" that defines life inside the gates. Our consulting experience has shown that these cultural attributes hold their predictive value no matter where you are in the world. For example, high levels of procedural justice or management credibility correlate to better performance just as much in China as they do in The Netherlands or Brazil. More importantly, a culture with these attributes is owned and driven by leadership, not by some outside national or historical force. What does differ is the way in which leaders need to develop these cultural characteristics as well as the practices of safety generally. Put another way, the "what" of safety is the same everywhere. It is the "how" that changes. For example, identifying workplace exposures is an important aspect of safety performance everywhere, but how that is done can change with the regional culture (e.g.,

The "what" of safety is the same everywhere. It is the "how" that changes.

peer-to-peer observations or superior-subordinate observations). One of the biggest challenges for any leader who has not "grown up" in the culture in which he or she is working is to understand why people are doing what they do. Excellent leaders take time to understand the "why" behind the culture and do not make assumptions about a person's beliefs or intellect to relieve themselves of accepting responsibilities for the outcomes.

In the rush of day-to-day work life, it is easy to make assumptions about what is important or not. We can mistake success in one area for success in safety generally, such as when organizations assume good personal safety data represents good functioning in all types of safety.[2] On a practical level, the inability to "connect the dots" of safety's parts and principles leads to dangerous organizational inconsistencies. Sometimes the isolation is so subtle as to be invisible unless you were to look for it, e.g., when exposure data are excluded from business decisions. Regardless, the result is the same; organizations continue to place significant investments of time and resources into singular solutions that by themselves never quite add up to a whole.

SHARED PRINCIPLES

The leader's job is to understand, first, what needs to happen for safety performance to improve and, second, to engage employees in that work. Safety practices such as identifying exposures, the use of controls, data reporting, and so on retain their value everywhere. But how these things are implemented does and should change according to local needs, culture, type of processes, exposures, and other considerations unique to the work being done. The point is being able to tell the difference between the "what" and the "how" in all aspects of safety.

At a basic level, safety can be defined as the prevention of harm to people, property, and the environment. This goal is what all safety efforts, regardless of industry, aim toward. Although it is tempting to think about the various kinds of safety as being very different, they all share fundamental underlying elements that are critical to gaining an understanding of how to improve.

Exposure

Accidents of any type are a direct result of exposure to hazards. By "exposure" we mean any condition, decision, behavior, activity, cultural standard, process, or system (or lack thereof) that creates a probability of an accident. Exposure is a risk unquantified, but able to be influenced up or down. Exposures are present at the intersection of people, processes, systems, and equipment—and these intersections are not limited to the shop floor. For instance, leaders can create exposure through their decisions (or lack thereof) and work processes can inadvertently encourage behaviors, such as shortcuts or workarounds, that put employees in harm's way. Put positively, decisions can be made and work processes designed that actually reduce exposure at the shop floor and make accidents less likely.

---

2   Notably, the separation of process safety and personal safety activities is a frequent theme in the investigation of catastrophic events.

Leadership

No matter what their functional area, leaders set the priorities and determine the tone with which things are done in an organization. Through what they say, what they choose to focus on, and what they do, leaders can make safety functioning easy or hard. They determine the quality of organizational and safety systems, and thus have the power to create a high-performing, and safety-friendly, culture. Among organizations affected by safety incidents, we commonly see leaders without a strong understanding of safety leadership and how it relates to overall organizational leadership. Instead, we often see the responsibility for safety improvement delegated to technical professionals who do not have the line position nor the training, support, or skills required to effect the organizational changes necessary for improvement. This makes the task faced by the safety professional—whether he or she is targeting transportation safety, patient safety, worker safety, or process safety—extremely challenging.

Good safety leadership and good leadership are interconnected. It is very difficult to be one without being the other. Safety has the potential to serve as a powerful platform for exhibiting leadership and building the organizational characteristics that lead to overall high performance.

Systems

Adverse events in any field can result from complex processes embedded in the organization, not just from the actions of an individual employee. A key characteristic of all safety issues is that they are influenced by more than just technical root causes. When equipment fails, why does it fail? If someone takes a shortcut and doesn't follow a procedure, why does that happen? If maintenance practices fail, what is the cause? If you examined every safety incident of any consequence, you are likely to find root causes that relate to both hardware (equipment and facilities) and "software" (meaning, in this context, the behavior of both front-line workers and managers/supervisors). Root causes may be removed in both time and place from the location of an incident. This is equally true when one investigates an airplane crash or a refinery fire or a fall from a scaffold.

Culture

Culture—the way we do things around here—refers to the shared, often unconscious values, attitudes, standards, and assumptions that govern behavior, especially in situations that lack clearly defined rules and procedures. To appreciate the importance of organizational culture to safety, consider how often accidents occur in situations in which employees deviate from procedure or in which procedures are weakly defined or nonexistent. Culture, along with motivation and context, also influences the mindset that employees bring to safety activities in general. It is almost a cliché that in organizations struggling with safety, employees at all levels tend to view regulatory compliance as a burden. Yet it's no less true that these views are a function of the culture in which they work, the signals they receive from leaders about what's valued, and the systems that define the work. The interrelationship among those three factors can cause two locations doing the same work with the same equipment and the same safety systems to have very different outcomes. Even when the safety systems are highly specified by regulations (as, for example, in U.S. coal mines), the safety records of different organizations differ greatly because of the impact of leadership and culture. This is equally true when comparing the rate of healthcare-acquired infection among hospital patients.

Best Practice: Make a Connection

A few years ago one of our consultants began work with a large manufacturing organization in Asia. The CEO said the right words about safety and directed his people to "do the right thing," but in reality he was too busy jetting around the world finalizing acquisitions and being a CEO to really know what was going on at the plant level. His direct reports adopted the CEO's detached approach and effectively left safety matters entirely to the safety manager several levels below them. As our consultant's work with this company progressed, the consultant spent quite a bit of time with the CEO and finally convinced him to take the time to actually walk through one of his plants. Although the CEO's staff had reserved just an hour of his tightly scheduled time for the visit, the CEO ended up spending several hours on the floor engaging workers in animated conversation. Leaving the plant at the end of the day, the CEO turned to our consultant to thank him for suggesting the idea. "I learned more about my business today," he said, "than I have during my whole tenure as CEO."

This CEO's experience is actually very common. Many leaders and executives find their assumptions being challenged when they engage the topic of worker safety in a real way. Many are quite surprised and deeply moved to discover that the state of safety is inherently tied to the operational excellence of the business itself, and that they can actually do something to improve both.

COMMON PATTERNS IN SAFETY DEVELOPMENT

Later in this book we describe in detail the disciplines that reflect these common principles and that underlie all types of safety. While it is commonplace in safety to describe advancements in binary terms (something is there or it is not, something is "good" or "bad"), we have found that it is more accurate to describe the experience of improvement in stages. The underlying principles of all types of safety are not static switches that are either on or off. They are fluid states that have discernible stages of progression—from the dormant to the fully actualized. Further, as a fluid state, it is quite possible to regress as well as progress.

The purpose of the Zero Index framework we present here is to capture these disciplines and describe them in a way that helps leaders, regardless of industry, application, or situation, understand the essential elements of their success. More important, our aim is to help leaders understand where they are on this continuum and what improvement looks like.

> **In your organization, is safety performance seen as something externally imposed or internally valued?**

The transformations we have seen in organizations are a lot like the changes you see in people who undertake a fitness regimen. One person may be in fairly good shape and decide to make the changes on her own. Another might be suffering from illness (or is worried about injury) and feels better about starting the new regimen with advice from his doctor. No matter their starting points, there is a common pattern of development in various aspects of people's engagement with the new practices. The same is true in organizations. Most notably, when organizations undertake a safety transformation, we see changes in the locus of control, coherence, and posture.

The Locus of Control

The more fluent organizations become in safety performance, the less they see safety as an externally imposed mandate and the more they adopt safety practices as an internal imperative. Organizations at the low end of the safety performance spectrum tend to express safety in terms of rules, requirements, and consequences (usually negative)—all things outside of the individuals' or organization's control. Safety activities are focused on meeting the demands of these external forces, such as regulatory agencies, governmental bodies, or public opinion; as a result, safety is largely detached from the mission of the organization. High-performing organizations, on the other hand, embody a sense of self-determination. Safe work is a part of who they are and something they choose to do. The standards they strive to meet are their own and usually exceed those set by outside bodies. In between, we see organizations in various stages of development straddling the line between external and internal drivers; for example, trying to engage employees in safety for its own sake while still measuring success against regulatory metrics.

Coherence

In low-performing organizations, safety functions and disciplines exist in isolation, often conflicting or nullifying each other. Not surprisingly, these efforts require tremendous energy just to maintain momentum. Here you will often see organizations express safety in terms of a dichotomy: it's "either" safety "or" production. As organizations begin to advance in the disciplines, they notice that the boundaries between safety and business begin to dissolve. Safety becomes something that helps the organization meet its goals; safety practices complement other business functions; business and safety cohere. Safety is no longer an onerous burden to be met at the lowest possible cost. At the highest levels of functioning, the potential for safety to engage employees at a human level becomes not just an idea but an actuality.

> In your organization, how integrated are safety systems with each other and with the business at large?

Posture

For years, many in the safety field have talked about being proactive instead of reactive, particularly with regard to the organization's response to injuries. Proactivity is a good thing, of course; but the elements of safety functioning, which include systems, culture, and leadership, are far more complex. Posture can be static, backwards looking, or forward oriented. It is not just about the timing of safety-related action; it is a reflection of the degree of involvement, awareness, and intent that directs that action. Organizations that progress in safety typically move from a passive state (at the low end), in which injuries and their contributing factors "just happen", to an active state (at the highest end), in which leaders seek out opportunities for optimization and improvement across a wide range of factors.

CREATING A COMMON APPROACH

Ultimately, an organization's safety transformation is not just about practice but also about mindset. The more adept the organization becomes at the practice of safety, the less the organization views safety as a burden imposed by others, and the more safety is valued for its own sake. Similarly, just as an athlete can get stuck at a certain stage of fitness, perhaps no longer resisting the new exercise regimen and better diet but not continuously upgrading their program, organizations can also get stuck at a certain level of performance on their journey forward. The purpose of the Zero Index model is to help you detect and diagnose your stage and monitor your progression forward.

While the various focus points of safety have differing characteristics, both in terms of how they are executed and how we react to them, the discussion in this chapter shows that there are fundamental commonalities whenever safety is a consideration. A common approach to safety improvement is indeed possible. In future chapters we describe a holistic model that addresses the interactions among people, equipment, management systems/procedures, reinforcement systems, leadership, and culture, and how those interactions lead to excellence in safety, with specifics tailored to the types of risk being targeted. Having such a holistic model allows us to approach safety at a more fundamental level, to facilitate the exchange of best practices among areas of safety now seen as different, and to design safety improvement efforts that simultaneously address multiple types of safety outcomes. This is the function and purpose of the Zero Index model.

A common approach to safety improvement is indeed possible.

NOTES

NOTES

REFRAMING OUR ASSUMPTIONS ABOUT SAFETY

by Kristen J. Bell

REFRAMING OUR ASSUMPTIONS ABOUT SAFETY

When human beings are presented with a challenge, we typically rely on our experience and what we know—an accepted set of assumptions or guidelines—to respond to that challenge. These assumptions and guidelines can be individual and personal, or they can be shared among members of an organization. When they are shared, they don't just constrain one person's thinking, they can also put limits on what an organization can achieve. In our work around the world, BST has discovered that among the biggest challenges to safety advancement are the artificial parameters that constrain organizational thinking about safety performance.

Some constraints are helpful, because they trigger desirable behavior. When people assume that meetings always start on time, they are more likely to arrive on time, which contributes to a high-functioning, efficient organization. When workers assume that good things happen when their project comes in below budget, and bad things happen when it doesn't, they are more likely to optimize their resources.

Unfortunately, other guidelines, spoken or unspoken, are not always as helpful. When employees assume that reporting an injury will result in some form of retaliation, they are unlikely to share injury information with people who could help eliminate the exposure. When managers assume that they can assess exposure by examining injury statistics alone, they are not likely to seek the kind of information needed to make good decisions. Arguably, the most harmful assumptions are broad generalizations that constrain management's views of the organization, its people, or its challenges. Incorrect assumptions can be limiting—and dangerous.

REFRAMING ASSUMPTIONS

Reframing is a technique for putting fixed ideas in a new context in order to see them in a new way. It helps replace unhelpful assumptions with more constructive ones and opens one's mind to new possibilities. We've begun to reveal the harm of limited or false assumptions in chapters 1 and 2. Here are four common assumptions that constrain organizational thinking about safety performance and prevent us from becoming a Zero Index organization—followed by a reframing of each.

Old Assumption 1: Being Ahead Means Being in Front

Organizations that have led the way in safety can be vulnerable to the mistaken assumption that their past successes have put them so far in the lead that there is nothing they can learn from others. They are so used to paving the way for others that they have forgotten they are not alone. Because they think they've already achieved perfection, safety improvement is a journey with no roadmap—there's nowhere to travel. They see themselves as working productively and profitably without harming a soul in the process, yet they feel as if they are alone. Because no other organization has better safety results, they think they have to keep inventing new tactics for safety improvement.

Is a star professional athlete so good at her sport that she has to constantly invent new moves to get better? Of course not. The athlete improves her game by developing her strength, speed, and agility and by practicing the fundamentals of the sport with her team. If flexibility is holding her back, she needs to resolve that in order to become stronger. As she improves her individual abilities, her team adjusts to her. As her team improves, she adjusts her own play. If the athlete loses touch with her team, she is still capable of becoming stronger, quicker, and more skilled—but she'll weaken her team's performance.

Instead of inventing new tactics, focus on the fundamentals. In a similar way, organizations that are leading the way in safety need to keep strengthening the fundamentals, improving what they already do well and eliminating barriers to improvement. Rather than inventing new tactics, though, they would be better off focusing on the fundamentals and adapting them to their situation.

Reframed: Organizations excel by honing and refining proven tactics more effectively than anyone else. In other words, Joe doesn't need a fancy new gold-plated whistle; instead, he needs to pay better attention to what's going on around him—and then blow the whistle already in his hand.

Old Assumption 2: Improve Safety Programs and Results Will Follow

Actually, most of the organizations we work with already have reasonably good safety programs—often excellent safety programs. The tendency to build, expand, or add new programs on top of old ones can create an unwieldy accumulation of poorly integrated programs that consume a great deal of management and employee resources.

Are safety programs seen as the be all and end all in your organization? One way to tell is by reviewing your organization's safety goals. (If your managers are accountable just for safety outcomes and not for eliminating exposures, then you have far greater safety challenges, and worrying about too great a focus on safety programs doesn't even apply to you—yet.) If the safety goals say that your managers are accountable for something like the "completion of planned safety improvements, completion of safety training, implementation of fatality prevention protocols, implementation of corrective actions resulting from health, safety, and environment (HSE) audits," or something similar, then the safety-program-will-fix-everything assumption may be limiting your success.

An organization is a dynamic system with inputs, outputs, outcomes, and feedback loops among its various components. Because the parts of the system depend on one another, changing one part affects the others. If a company decides to manufacture a new part, it will not only have to create a new work flow encompassing materials procurement to shipping, but will also have to deal with financial and legal implications, changes to hiring, training, and performance management systems. It may have labor relations issues, and the culture may be affected. Supervisors will need to monitor and provide feedback on different behaviors. During this whole process the company could be removing old exposures to risk while creating entirely new ones. Therefore, focusing on just one part of the organizational system at a time is insufficient. Whatever the organizational objective—safety or otherwise—managers need to understand the organizational dynamics and devise solutions that ensure alignment among the various working parts.

Related to this is the false assumption that safety needs to be managed as a separate enterprise. Nowhere is this more prominent than in the area of process safety, which too often is managed separately from not only operations but also from personnel safety. The Baker Report, released two years after the 2005 Texas City oil refinery disaster, stated:

> "The Panel found instances of a lack of operating discipline, toleration of serious deviations from safe operating practices, and apparent complacency toward serious process safety risks..."

Gaps like these arise, in part, when process safety is segregated from other aspects of business functioning. The elements of process safety are largely engineering focused, addressing the design, operation, and maintenance of chemical-using processes. Process safety has its own procedures, training, incident investigation, permit programs, pre-startup reviews, and so forth. Clearly, it's important to have tactics focused on specific problems, issues, or goals (including process safety). However, tactics alone will not establish a healthy, dynamic system in which the various parts are aligned and mutually supportive. What's more, tactics can be relegated to a few individuals, which can be extremely dangerous. Failing to engage every individual in an organization in the mission to minimize exposure creates the potential for conflicting goals and priorities as well as significant communication gaps. The Baker Report illustrates this well:

> "A substantial gulf appears to have existed, however, between the actual performance of BP's process safety management systems and the company's perception of that performance."

We're not suggesting that safety should disappear into the fabric of the organization—we're just saying it needs to be addressed in a broader, more integrated way. It doesn't mean there shouldn't be safety meetings, safety training, or specific activities focused on safety. It means that safety shouldn't be relegated to the domain of the safety professionals. Instead, every individual in the organization must have goals and objectives that support the organization's value for safety. Every individual must approach every aspect of their work with a certain consciousness about identifying and minimizing exposure.

Does your organization focus on tactics instead of creating an integrated objective?

Reframed: Safety needs to be managed as an integrated objective in which every individual has a role and every system and process is aligned with the organization's objectives. In other words, safety isn't Joe's job—it's everybody's job.

Old assumption 3: Leadership Development is the Key to Improved Organizational and Safety Functioning.

Over the last decade, organizations have become increasingly more sophisticated in their understanding of the role of leadership in safety. Rather than reinforcing the "prescribe and allocate" maxim of good leadership, the research reveals that specific leadership behaviors actively shape an organization's success in safety improvement. In a series of studies BST conducted starting in the 1990s, we learned that while the average improvement in safety performance following implementation of our proprietary behavior-based safety improvement process amounted to about 25% in the first year, some clients—those in the top quartile of performance—achieved even better results, a 40% improvement, on average, in the first year. When we compared the top implementations to the average implementations, leadership was consistently identified as the deciding factor. In 2004, when we added a leadership component to our behavior-based safety process, sites using our methodology achieved an average 40% improvement in their first year. So we are certain that leadership is important.

Figure 3–1

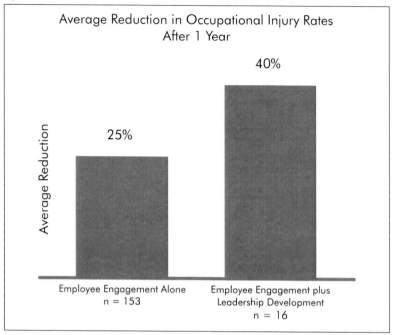

Results from a 2004 study showing injury rate reduction in companies using an employee engagement process alone versus those using employee engagement plus leadership development.

Unfortunately, these study results (Figure 3–1) have been misinterpreted. All too often, people conclude, "It's all about leadership development. If we send our leaders through training, then we, too, will see a 40% improvement in our safety performance." This is not true. It's important to understand that these results have been achieved in the context of the implementation of a specific behavior-based safety process. Leaders were not just developing their leadership skills in the classroom, they were immediately applying them to a safety improvement process in which they had a crucial, defined role. The difference is in the application of the leadership practices and in leadership engagement: skills development is a tactic we use to help make those things possible.

What are the operative safety assumptions in your organization?

Reframed: The key to excellent organizational functioning comes from the successful application of leadership practices and leadership engagement—not shipping Joe off to leadership camp.

Old Assumption 4: Those Who Have the Power to Make Change Happen are Those Who Should Define the Change

In fact, all kinds of problem-solving talent remains unused in organizations. Without question, those people who have the power to make change happen do have crucial responsibilities: defining the desired future state, understanding the current state, developing principles that will guide decisions in the change process, and defining the overall strategy for closing the gap. People farther down in the organization, however, are far better positioned to design the details and logistics of the implementation itself. Every change initiative faces all kinds of barriers, and the people who know best how to remove the barriers are those closest to them. Even if they lack the power to totally remove barriers, it would be a mistake not to involve them in the problem-solving process.

Reframed: Those who have the power to create change should lead the change; those most affected by the change should help define how to make the change happen. In other words, ask Joe how to get line workers to switch from ____ to ____—he's there every day. (Or: Joe should talk not just to the CEO but to the janitor.)

MAKING ROOM FOR WHAT'S NEXT

Our assumptions about safety performance dictate our execution, and ultimately, the functioning and outcomes that follow. By examining existing assumptions and reframing harmful ones, leaders can redefine what is possible and create an organization in which:

- There is a clear path towards safety improvement, no matter how much success you have had in the past;

- Safety is managed as an integrated objective in which every individual has a role and every system and process is aligned with the organization's objectives;

- All employees demonstrate leadership practices and are skillfully engaged in the safety improvement process, and;

- People who have the power to create change lead the change, while those who are most affected by the change help to define how to make the change happen.

In this chapter we examined the ways in which perceptions and thinking shape our reality. Removing the constraints on our thinking, understanding the barriers to successful execution, and reexamining old assumptions about safety performance all help to create a platform for defining a new way forward. In the next section, we will explore what can happen when organizations start to redefine what is possible.

NOTES

PART II:
The Art of What's Possible

INTRODUCING THE ZERO INDEX

by Colin Duncan

INTRODUCING THE ZERO INDEX

Whenever we set out to improve our performance, personally or professionally, we typically start by defining a goal. We might want to be more fit, master a new skill, or simply become better at what we do, and that goal serves to focus our efforts. But as most of us eventually discover along the way, a goal is really just the beginning. By itself, a goal doesn't tell us what it takes to achieve—or sustain—the new state. Sustained changes in performance demand a new way of thinking and acting. For example, becoming more fit requires doing the things that a fit person does (exercising, eating healthily) and doing them consistently and well; mastering a new skill (such as learning a language) requires integrating the new practice into our daily routine; and so on. In the end, the achieved goal is really an effect, not the substance, of the higher level of performance.

Advancing safety functioning is no different. We have learned from working at thousands of client sites around the world that a number by itself doesn't define extraordinary safety. Rather, it is the state of motion that does. The zero harm goal (sometimes called injury-free, or zero incidents) is certainly the right target. The problem is that it is so poorly defined that many organizations confuse having the goal (no harm to employees, customers, and community) for the activities that produce that effect. The result of this confusion is that these organizations exhaust themselves on the same practices and approaches they have always used and become frustrated when they realize the same level of results.

In chapter 1 we explored the history of safety performance, how we got where we are today, and began to reimagine what is possible. In chapter 2, we show the basic tenets of a safety framework common to all industry. In chapter 3, we learned that achieving a truly zero harm organization requires stepping back from our existing ideas and assumptions, reframing our thinking, and recognizing the limits of existing approaches to safety performance. In this section, we flesh out the vision, posing the questions: What does a zero harm organization actually look like? What are its parts? How can zero harm performance be defined in terms that can be observed, measured—and, more important—achieved?

SAFETY AS A STRATEGY

Conventional safety thinking has focused largely on what we call safety systems—mechanisms that directly seek to reduce or remove exposure to hazards in the workplace. Supply the right systems, the thinking goes, and results will follow. Studies and experience, however, have shown this vision to be flawed; for example, different sites with practically identical safety systems are known to report very different incident frequency rates, even when weighted for technology and work forces.

As we mentioned in the introduction, Zero Index organizations are distinguished by their ability to take a big picture view of how safety performance occurs. Safety is not a program, but an integral business function that is influenced by, and in turn influences, operational execution. Zero Index performance is:

How close is your organization to zero harm?

- **Comprehensive:** Safety activities are guided by a detailed, granular strategy developed from a comprehensive understanding of the gap between where the organization is and where it desires to be.

- **Anticipatory:** Safety performance is driven by a sophisticated set of metrics that detect changes in exposure before they create events.

- **Externally and internally focused:** The organization adapts to changes that influence exposure within and outside the organization.

- **Integrated:** Safety activities are coordinated across functions; they complement other business systems and processes and show a high degree of skill and sophistication.

- **Risk based versus outcome based:** The measure of success (and the trigger for action) is exposure to injuries, not the occurrence of injuries themselves.

Continuing with our recap, achieving this level of performance is not easy. Nobody starts out as a Zero Index organization. As with all human endeavors, excellence in safety is achieved in stages.

The Zero Index model encompasses 10 practices, or disciplines (to be described in chapters 5, 6, and 7) that define safety performance (Figure 4-1).

Figure 4-1. The Zero Index.

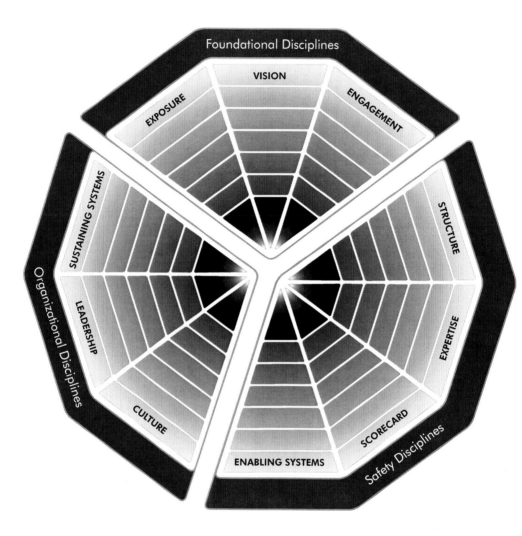

Performance of these practices can be roughly grouped into low, average, and high levels, depending on the sophistication and fluency with which the organization applies the disciplines. We refer to these low, medium, and high levels as Avoidance-driven, Compliance-driven, and Values-driven, each of which has two stages. Together they make up a developmental continuum of the six stages of safety functioning (Figure 4–2):

Figure 4–2. The continuum of safety functioning.

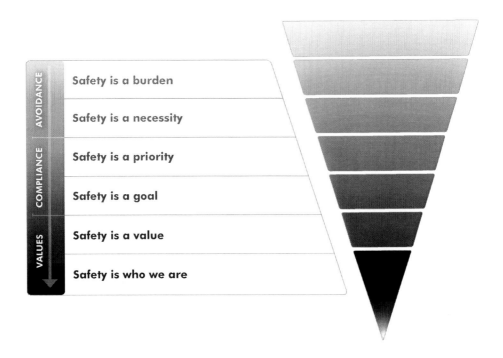

The Avoidance-Driven Organization

Avoidance-driven organizations are defined by the underlying view that safety is an unwelcome requirement, a nuisance—even, in some unfortunate cases, a hindrance to the running of the business. This viewpoint is reflected in the development and execution of safety systems and practices and their relationship to the rest of the business. *The driving focus of Avoidance organizations is cost.* Leaders often equate minimal outlay on accidents and fines with good safety performance.

In these organizations, the investment in safety of individuals, teams, and the organization itself is minimal; those involved in safety, whether in oversight or technical roles, tend to be viewed as enforcers of external regulations rather than as partners in helping the business realize its goals. Safety is largely seen as a requirement imposed from outside, with outcomes that are largely beyond the organization's (or the individual's) control.

In an Avoidance organization, the safety systems that do exist are isolated from the business and from each other. Safety outcomes tend to be viewed as disconnected from other elements of the business and safety activities are restricted to the necessary. As a result, blame and reaction are common and the culture tends to be highly fragmented between levels and workgroups.

Avoidance-driven organizations have two distinct stages of functioning, defined by how the organization views the role of safety performance in the business:

- **Safety is a burden.** At this first stage, safety is predominantly seen as something imposed on the organization by external bodies and the outcomes are largely regarded as something outside the organization's control. It's common at this stage to hear leaders describe accidents as "inevitable"; and employees may describe safety as "management's job." At this stage, many foundational elements of safety functioning, such as a safety professional and governance, may be nonexistent because they may not be seen as required. Safety-related activities tend to be reactive.

- **Safety is a necessity.** At the next stage of Avoidance functioning, safety is viewed as a necessity that must be managed. Most of the basic elements of safety functioning have started to appear, yet are largely anemic and ineffective. Safety activities tend to be siloed. Engagement is minimal and is largely pushed rather than pulled. People do things because they have to, not because they want to.

The Compliance-Driven Organization

Compliance-driven organizations are characterized by change. As opposed to Avoidance organizations, where safety tends to be viewed as an externally imposed mandate, Compliance organizations consider safety to have some intrinsic value to the organization, albeit in

Compliance organizations are reactive and goal-driven.

a limited way. The predominant mode in a Compliance-driven organization is improvement. The focus is on reducing injuries, and objectives advance as functioning improves.

Unlike Avoidance organizations, in which safety activity is driven by the need to avoid problems, Compliance organizations appear highly active by comparison. An improvement focus means activity, and fundamental safety systems and practices, such as the role of safety expertise, governance, safety-enabling systems, and metrics, are all discernibly present, if not always effective. Compliance-driven leaders may not have a sophisticated under-standing of safety performance, but they pay attention to it and may even take on some role in directing its execution. The emphasis on improvement, combined with a limited view of safety's value to the organization, often means that little attention is paid to how safety systems are aligned with the wider functioning of the business.

The two stages of functioning in Compliance-driven organizations reflect a growing value for safety:

- **Safety is a priority.** As safety shifts from a regulatory necessity to something of value to the organization, the predominant mode is on taking action. Leaders in these organizations recognize the importance of safety and elevate its functioning to the level of priority. Lacking a formal mandate, however, safety at this stage still tends to be largely reactive.

- **Safety is a goal.** At this stage, the immediacy that comes from recognizing safety as a priority has matured into safety as an explicit goal, where safety is formally inc!uded as part of the oversight of senior leaders.

The Values-Driven Organization

In Values-driven organizations, safety is identity.

Values-driven organizations make up a small per-centage of organizations in industry and represent the highest levels of safety functioning. Values orga-nizations are characterized by their expansiveness. As opposed to Compliance-driven organizations, where the focus is on internal improvement, Values-driven organizations have internalized safety to the point where safety characterizes the functioning of the organization. The predominant mode in a Values organization is safety as identity. The focus is on exposure reduction and integration. Fundamental safety systems and practices, such as the safety expertise, safety decision making and structure, safety-enabling systems, and metrics are all functioning at high levels. Values-driven leaders have a sophisticated understanding of safety performance and include safety in strategic decision making. Fluency in safety as a strategy and an inherent understanding of safety's place in the wider fabric of the organization give Values-driven organizations the agility to quickly adapt to and execute change.

Values-driven organizations have two distinct stages of functioning:

- **Safety is a value.** While the word value is frequently used to indicate what an organization aspires to, here we mean what the organization actually embodies. That is, worker wellbeing and health are recognized as having intrinsic worth, irrespective of their other benefits. Safety-related decisions, structure, and activities are oriented toward the pursuit of safety for its own sake.

- **Safety is who we are.** At this highest level, safety is internalized as a value and has become part of the identity of individuals and the organization. The organization is highly sensitive to even subtle changes in exposure and employees take the initiative to partner across traditional boundaries to eliminate exposure.

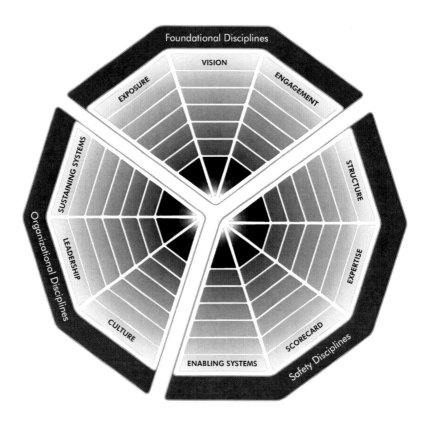

A NEW MODEL OF SAFETY EXECUTION

The six stages of functioning outlined here—Burden, Necessity, Priority, Goal, Value, and Who we are—form a framework for understanding safety performance beyond "high" and "low." The Zero Index model allows us to discern in broad terms how the highest level of functioning looks, acts, and feels differently from the lowest level—and how the stages in between differ from each other. At the same time, we need a model that does more than catalogue organizational traits. To chart a path forward, we need a model that is sufficiently granular to be actionable. It needs to identify specific characteristics at each stage of functioning and define them in sufficient detail that leaders and safety professionals can assess their current state and identify exactly where they can go next. To achieve excellence, we need to know what it looks like and how to achieve it, avoiding the oversimplifications that have ground many good ideas into meaningless platitudes.

In the next few chapters, we will fill out this six-stage framework with the 10 disciplines (left) that together drive safety functioning and determine an organization's level of performance.

When we use the word *discipline* in this context, we simply mean a set or system of concepts or constructs—in this case, disciplines that support the health and safety of employees. Just as the framework is a continuum, so too are the parts, which flow in distinctly identifiable stages. In chapters 5, 6, and 7 we define these disciplines and discuss their unique progression within the Zero Index framework.

NOTES

THE FOUNDATIONAL DISCIPLINES

by Theodore D. Apking, Ph.D.

THE FOUNDATIONAL DISCIPLINES

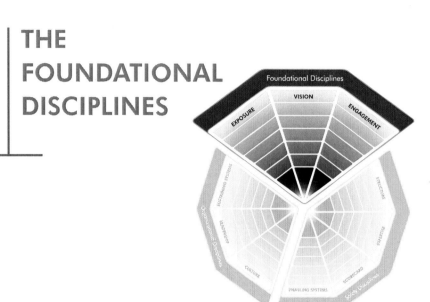

Following the space shuttle Columbia disaster in 2003, in which the crew of seven perished during reentry, the board investigating the accident identified significant organizational issues contributing to the disaster. Among them was an overreliance on past success, a lack of integrated management across program elements, and an informal chain of command that operated outside the organization's rules. The National Aeronautics and Space Administration (NASA) asked our firm to assist in the development and implementation of a plan for changing the culture and safety climate of the agency. We began our work by conducting a thorough assessment. What we found was an organization in transition.

Employees had a strong can-do spirit that reflected a proud legacy of achievement. At the same time, the agency knew it had to create a culture that valued safety, people, and integrity, in addition to excellence. Individually, people showed a strong commitment to safety, but open communication about safety issues was not the norm. People didn't feel respected or valued, and often learned that the raising of negative issues, however important, was not welcomed. With many ongoing initiatives, people lacked a clear sense of "how it all fit together." So NASA employees naturally defaulted to what they had always done and done well: they focused on technical achievement. Perhaps not surprisingly, this situa-

The problem at NASA was not one of know-how. The agency employed some of the brightest people in the world.

tion reinforced the "cultural traits and organizational practices detrimental to safety" pointed to by the Columbia Accident Investigation Board.[1]

The problem was not one of know-how. The agency employed some of the brightest people in the world who could certainly figure out how to "do" safety. The problem was rather that, at the operational level, the agency's mindset about what it meant to be a technological giant was overshadowing the development of a clear and meaningful role for safety excellence.

In any area of performance, the rules and beliefs that govern our action and thinking determine the scope of our effort, the choices we make, and ultimately, the outcomes we achieve. In sports training, coaches counter this effect by getting athletes to visualize optimal performance. In choirs, choral directors sometimes instruct performers who are prone to singing flat notes to "think high." Picturing success is a way of defining what's possible and how to get there. Without that picture, an athlete may be limited to her immediate experience, or how he currently sees himself, and will perform only to that level. And the altos may persistently sing off-key.

What are your beliefs about safety?

In safety, the three Foundational disciplines—Vision, Engagement, and Exposure—operate in much the same way. These disciplines create the mind set with which we approach safety, shaping how we talk about and engage in safety activities. From our direct client experience and from our extensive research on organizational culture, we know that employees' attitudes about safety are affected by their leaders' beliefs and rules. This is true because leaders create and manage the procedures and policies that affect workers on the job every day.

- **Vision** refers to how senior-most leaders articulate and define the organization's aims with respect to safety. This discipline focuses on how the organization's activities and strategies reflect the value the organization places on safety, and the degree to which the organization is motivated to improve safety.

- **Engagement** describes the extent to which leaders in the organization invest themselves in safety, as reflected in the culture and the value placed on people and relationships. The greater the value leaders place on people and relationships, the greater the value employees place on safety.

---

1 Columbia Accident Investigation Board, *Columbia Accident Investigation Board Report* (August 2003), vol.1, p. 9. Available at www.nasa.gov.

- **Exposure** refers to how the organization's senior-most leaders think about injury causation. Their views about causation influence the comprehensiveness and effectiveness of exposure-reduction efforts.

Individually and collectively, these three Foundational disciplines set the stage for all activities related to safety performance improvement and indirectly influence the probability that those activities will be successful. In the case of NASA, lack of cohesion in the agency's mindset cascaded down to the operational level as conflicting messages when the stated values (such as safety and people) clashed with what was actually rewarded (meeting schedule and budget).

All 10 of our safety disciplines exist on a continuum, with different organizations falling at various places on the discipline scales, from Avoidance-driven, to Compliance-driven, to Values-driven. If a company's performance is high— or low—what are the implications for that organization and its employees?

THE VISION DISCIPLINE

When the leaders of a company (or unit) articulate their vision for safety, they begin to shape the strategies that their respective managers and supervisors will follow and the actions they will take. As we know from decades of psychological research, individual and group behavior tends to match the expectations or goals that have been set—no more or no less. This, of course, assumes that the individuals possess the capabilities to meet the vision and that no immediately negative consequences arise as a result of fulfilling the vision.

We all know that goals are important—they guide our behavior and say something about what we value or hold dear. We probably all know someone who has made it his or her personal goal to run a marathon. Competing in a marathon is an extremely challenging activity that requires a high level of physical fitness, which can be achieved only by engaging in a well-planned exercise regime over an extended period. Similarly, a goal of zero harm in safety puts into motion a rigorous process to minimize exposure. Like the goal of running a marathon, zero harm sets expectations for behavior and achievement that cannot be taken lightly. Merely setting the goal to run a marathon says something about the value that the runner places on having a healthy body and on achieving a high level of fitness.

Reflecting the Value Placed on Safety

The way in which an organization's senior-most leaders describe an organization's vision for safety is truly important, because it influences the way

Setting a goal of zero harm puts into motion a rigorous process.

people in the organization think about safety and affects their motivation to improve it. The Vision discipline, like all 10 of the Zero Index disciplines, runs along a continuum. Organizations performing at the low (Avoidance-driven) end do only what is necessary in order to avoid large costs. Organizations at

the high (Values-driven) end minimize exposure to risk for employees and contractors by partnering with everyone who interacts with the organization: not just employees but customers, contractors, and the community in which the business resides.

We discover something when we reflect on the two extremes—leaders who just avoid costs versus those who do whatever is necessary to reduce exposure. Simply said, in the former situation, it is reasonable to conclude that money is most important; whereas in the latter, people are most important. The implications of these competing visions are enormous when it comes to the actions that people in the organization will (or will not) take to improve safety. Managers and supervisors, like everyone, endeavor to successfully meet expectations; furthermore, they hold others accountable for actions consistent with the visions that have been set. Behavior tends to match expectations.

When we visit a client organization, we evaluate the company's performance of the Vision discipline. Is the company avoidant when it comes to safety—only discussing it after high-cost accidents occur? We would categorize that company at the bottom of the continuum, in Avoidance-driven territory (Table 5–1). Or is the company proactive about safety, expressing lofty goals in an effort to decrease employee injuries? (If the goals are unrealistic and limited only to employees, that puts the company at the middle, or Compliance-driven, stage.) Or is the company wise enough to invest in integrating and optimizing the safety function so that exposure is minimized for everyone who interacts with the organization? We categorize that company's performance of the Vision discipline as the highest possible stage, making it a Values-driven company. And hats off to them!

TABLE 5–1. The Vision Discipline.
How the organization articulates or defines its goals with respect to safety.

	Facet	Defined as
AVOIDANCE	Avoidant	Avoid large costs.
	Minimalistic	Don't get caught failing to comply with government regulations.
COMPLIANCE	Responsive	Improve injury rates.
	Proactive	Avoid recordable injuries for employees or contractors.
VALUES	Progressive	Minimize exposure for employees and contractors.
	Universal	Minimize exposure for employees and contractors by partnering with everyone who interacts with the organization: customers, contractors, and the community.

What you might see or hear

Leaders will discuss safety only when it disrupts production. Citations and fines are seen as "the cost of doing business." When high-dollar accidents occur, there is plenty of blame to go around.

Leaders discuss safety infrequently and tend to frame it as a requirement. The organization's safety investment is in compliance tools and training. Safety-related decisions are based on avoiding regulatory penalties.

Leaders may express lofty goals that don't match reality. The organization's investment focuses on programs. Safety-related decisions are based on the likelihood of injury.

Leaders discuss safety performance as it actually is and frame the organization's goals with respect to closing perceived gaps. The organization extends programs and requirements to contractors. Safety-related decisions are based on coverage.

Leaders consider all injuries as preventable. The organization's investment in safety is focused on understanding and addressing risk. Safety-related decisions are based on exposure.

Leaders discuss safety as a sustainability issue. The organization's safety investment is in optimizing and integrating the safety function. Business decisions are based on their impact on safety.

As leaders formulate their organization's vision for safety, it is imperative that they consider the message that their vision sends to employees and all other stakeholders. In our experience, every hugely successful safety performance improvement process starts with a goal that motivates people to take action to reduce exposure for themselves and others. The message must be clear and unambiguous: It is everyone's job to take action so that, as one client put it, "Nobody gets hurt." A well-crafted and clearly articulated vision is essential to the creation of a healthy safety climate.

Evaluating the Vision Discipline

You can assess your own organization's performance of the Vision discipline by paying attention to your company's explicit and implicit objectives with regard to safety. Ask yourself:

- What is our vision for safety? Do we have one documented?

- How is the vision established?

- Which do we emphasize—injury rate or exposure reduction?

- What is safety's role in the wider business?

- Is safety executed in a way that matches our explicit (stated) vision? If not, what is our real focus?

- Are leadership priorities fairly static? Or are they always changing?

- Would people at various levels be able to articulate our vision for safety?

- What things compete with our vision for attention? For example, have production concerns ever preempted actions that support the safety vision?

- How do we resolve perceived conflicts between our safety vision and other business goals?

CASE IN POINT: VISION

Singapore's Workplace Safety & Health Strategy

The city-state of Singapore is home to more than five million people. It's also an industrial powerhouse where major organizations in shipping and logistics, construction, oil and gas, chemicals, finance, and manufacturing converge. In 2008, leaders from Singapore's major industry sectors joined with government, union, and academic leaders to form the Workplace Safety and Health (WSH) Council. In partnership with the Ministry of Manpower, the WSH Council launched a long-term, strategic plan for the nation's workplace safety and health practices. The plan, titled WSH: 2018, calls for reducing the national fatality rate to less than 1.8 per 100,000 workers by 2018. If reached, this goal would make Singapore one of the safest places to work in the world.

The detailed plan lays out four outcomes for Singaporean industry to achieve by 2018: reduce incident rates, make safety and health an integral part of business, establish Singapore's reputation as a center of workplace safety and health excellence, and establish a "progressive and pervasive" safety and health culture. The plan also lays out four specific strategies to achieve these ends.

WSH 2018 has led to numerous initiatives that target specific industry needs. Some programs focus on "hot spot" issues such as working at heights and in confined spaces, others help businesses develop fluency in or assist in the development of safety professionals. Officials say Singapore's ambitious vision for safety has driven an increase in safety-related activity across industry. Over 300,000 people are now trained in safety annually and more than 8,000 companies have embarked on WSH initiatives since the launch of the plan. While the country has yet to realize its 2018 vision, officials and leaders are already touting its impact. In 2010, Singapore realized its lowest fatality rate in six years, down 20% from the previous year.

Sources: American Society of Safety Engineers, "Workplace Safety and Health in Singapore," World Focus, 2011, 10 (3), p 10-17. WSH Council, "Singapore's Overall 2010 WSH Performance Improved, with Lowest Recorded Fatality Rate in 6 Years," 16 March 2011, www.wshc.sg.

THE ENGAGEMENT DISCIPLINE

Employees' underlying assumptions about the degree to which (and the ways in which) their leaders place a value on people and human relationships are key to safety. The greater the value leaders place on people and relationships (e.g., treating their employees like family members or friends), the greater the value employees place on safety-related activities in that organization. This makes intuitive sense—if the boss cares, we care, too. It is also validated by psychometric researchers who have studied the effect of a transformational leadership style on operational and safety performance. A transformational style can be loosely defined as "a leadership style that communicates a value for people and their development along with task completion." Leaders who adopt a transformational style routinely outperform leaders who fail to do so.

If the tone set in a company is that you do as you are told, you speak when spoken to, you don't collaborate, and you don't work in teams, then we see little engagement with or personal investment in safety—or in any other aspect of the enterprise, for that matter. People are not likely to risk getting involved with one another in this type of environment. On the other hand, consider a workplace in which leaders set a tone wherein helping each another become successful on the job is a shared responsibility and where people are encouraged by their supervisors to learn new skills, achieve their personal career goals, and help others to do the same. Coworkers generally feel like part of the family; their engagement with each other affects their engagement with safety.

Reflecting the Value Placed on People and Relationships

Several of our client organizations have developed this sense of family and personal ownership in a full-bodied manner, by taking advantage of this tone and promoting a caring work environment. In such a company, leaders describe a specific type of engagement in which "we are all our brother's keeper." This level of caring is specifically and behaviorally defined as an obligation—as a promise to intervene whenever any one employee sees someone else in harm's way. Technically, this is sometimes described as a willingness to approach others. Whether the situation is a worker engaging (or not) in a discussion about an observed risk or a leader taking interest (or not) in the personal success of a subordinate, it is easy to see the potential influence that a focus on people and human relationships can have on safety performance.

> To what degree is your organization a caring one?

Performance with the Engagement discipline runs the gamut (Table 5–2), from avoiding any effort on someone else's behalf (Avoidance-driven) to participating in strong partnerships throughout the organization (Values-driven).

NOTES

TABLE 5–2. The Engagement Discipline.
How the organization values people and relationships.

	Facet	Defined as
AVOIDANCE	Evasive	Employees and employers have no investment in one another. Each avoids effort to improve safety.
	Transactional	The organization views employees as an economic unit. Employees see the organization as a paycheck. Each does the minimum to get by in safety.
COMPLIANCE	Extrospective	Employees and employers are invested in safety improvement. Each sees progress as out of their control.
	Introspective	Managers see employees as their responsibility. Employees see themselves as cared for. Each sees how they can contribute to safety.
	Integrative	Managers and employees see each other as partners in improving safety, while taking personal responsibility for reducing exposure.
VALUES	Actualized	Employees' and employer's investment in safety transcends organizational boundaries. Each works to minimize exposure inside and outside the organization.

What you might see or hear

Employees in this organization are detached from the safety function. Safety is seen as a distraction (or an excuse to get out of work), and related activities tend to be avoided unless absolutely necessary. Mutual mistrust between employees and management prevents any significant collaboration on even basic safety issues.

The dominant transactional nature of relationships at this stage creates a quid-pro-quo stance toward safety engagement. Safety is frequently used as leverage for attaining other, more valued, objectives. Employees may express the belief that safety is "management's problem," and managers that accidents happen because employees "do stupid things."

Employees in organizations at this stage begin to demonstrate personal value for safety, but will have a high level of constraint recognition. Employees don't feel empowered to take action on their value for improvement, and will defer safety-related decisions (resources, shutting down equipment, etc.) to others. There may be frustration that "others" don't take safety seriously enough.

At this stage, ownership for safety begins to emerge as employees begin to connect personal value to action. Here you will often see employees volunteering for safety roles. Managers and leaders will ask questions about safety issues, trying to discover ways they might help.

The investment in safety deepens at the Integrative stage as employees and managers feel safe taking personal risk on behalf of safety. For example employees will take on leadership roles in safety activities and managers might take opportunities to mentor or coach employees in taking on these roles. Employees at all levels will report high levels of organizational support for safety.

At this stage, peoples' investment in safety supersedes implicit or explicit "ground rules." Managers and employees will routinely approach others for safety help, regardless of level or location. Communication about safety issues is spontaneous; employees will often offer ideas without being asked.

Leaders who employ an effective transformational leadership style are best equipped to build a work environment that is measured at the higher range of this scale or continuum. Simply said, leaders who help their employees become enthused about the future direction of the business, who behave in ways that earn employees' trust and respect, who challenge employees to explore new ways of thinking about old problems, and who build a feedback-rich workplace will experience the benefit of a highly-engaged workforce.

Evaluating the Engagement Discipline

To assess your organization's degree of Engagement, ask yourself:

- When it comes to work, what are employees and managers actually invested in?

- What drives participation in safety here?

- How do people see their role in safety?

- How do people explain safety outcomes? To what extent do they perceive they have the ability to make a positive difference?

- Do employees feel that the company genuinely cares about their safety?

- How likely are employees to raise safety concerns with each other or with management?

- How do employees and managers view each other? To what extent would they extend themselves to support the goals of the other?

CASE IN POINT: ENGAGEMENT

Personalizing Safety at PotashCorp

Relationships are a core element of life at PotashCorp, where senior leaders regularly visit sites to talk safety with employees. Company leaders focus on what they call "personalizing safety"; having open discussion with employees at all levels around exposure, culture, and day-to-day life. Leaders credit the approach with helping develop genuine enthusiasm for—and honest discussions about—safety issues.

A team made up of senior leaders meets regularly to discuss safety strategy, but the emphasis remains on making sure that safety involvement extends to every level. In recent years, that has meant defining more clearly the safety roles for supervisors and other leaders in addition to supporting ongoing employee-driven safety processes. In 2008 PotashCorp adopted what it calls the total safety approach, extending exposure reduction activities to anyone who "walks through the gate." One outcome of this philosophy is that contract employees now participate in safety activities and initiatives in the same way PotashCorp employees do. Since adopting that change, safety performance among the contractor population have seen a near 70% improvement.

The company's engagement approach is probably best embodied in its annual PotashCorp Day safety conference. Hosting 200 PotashCorp employees—nearly 10 people from every site in the organization—the event focuses on celebrating successes and setting the organization's sights on the challenges for the year ahead. Attendees include everyone from the CEO, COO, presidents, vice presidents, members of the board of directors to general managers and hourly safety process facilitators and steering team members.

PotashCorp also extends its networking outside, routinely hosting organizations looking for new ideas or to learn from the company's safety initiatives and practices. To PotashCorp leaders, networking is not just the right thing to do, it also gives employees exposure to new ideas. Senior director of safety and health Larry Simmons put the organization's success down to treating others with dignity and respect. "Throughout our organization, regardless of the position or level, our folks have developed a personal safety ethic that includes caring for others. This alignment is why you see the tremendous engagement from the board room to the shop floor."

THE EXPOSURE DISCIPLINE

The third and last Foundational discipline is Exposure, which refers to how organizational leaders think about injury causation. Beliefs about exposure directly influence the comprehensiveness and effectiveness of the activities associated with exposure reduction—if you truly don't believe something can be fixed, why bother even trying to fix it? The way we think about exposure can also affect the level of felt accountability among leaders and employees with regard to leading or participating in exposure-reduction efforts—if it's his job, not your job, why should you get involved? If we believe that injuries are almost always caused by people choosing to behave unsafely, we are unlikely to invest a lot of time and money investigating incidents and looking for root causes of those incidents, because deep inside we believe that we cannot stop people from choosing to behave unsafely—otherwise known as a "boys will be boys" attitude.

> **Do you believe that safety can improve in your organization?**

On the other hand, if we believe that injuries are a result of a complex combination of variables at the working interface[2] (our term for any place in which exposure to hazards is created, mitigated, or eliminated, and where adverse events occur or are prevented), and if we believe that people do not come to work planning to act in dangerous or unsafe ways, we have an entirely different appetite (and mindset) for investing time and money in the investigation of incidents and looking for the root causes of those incidents. If we as leaders see the world that way, we recognize that we must educate everyone in the organization about the role exposure plays in injury causation.

It is impossible for an individual to create an effective exposure-reduction process without giving some thought to understanding the history of incidents at the site and digging into the likely causes of those incidents. Fortunately, it is highly unusual today to find leaders in large, global companies who fall on the very low end of the Exposure discipline continuum. Thankfully, individuals who are not concerned with determining the root cause of injuries and are only focused on managing the aftermath as efficiently as possible so as not to disrupt production are rare birds in global organizations.

However, there is still much work to be done with this discipline. In our projects around the globe, we still encounter leaders who do not have a sophisticated understanding of injury causation. These leaders might be heard in private

---

2   The working interface specifically describes the configuration of people, process, and technology. This interface is where the work is done and safety is directly related to how well we reduce exposure here.

describing a recent incident and complaining that it resulted from workers doing something stupid. These leaders do not appreciate the multiple variables that interact to cause most incidents; they often hold the simplistic view that incidents are generally caused by the careless actions of workers, thereby limiting the range of factors that can even be considered in determining the cause of an incident. (If you think the accident was all Larry's fault, you're unlikely to wholeheartedly and open-mindedly explore the workload, processes, technology, and equipment maintenance in Larry's division.) This leadership nearsightedness directly reduces the odds that the root cause will ever actually be identified and reduces the impact of any possible solutions that could have been created to reduce workplace injuries.

The working interface is any environment in which exposure to hazards is created, mitigated, or eliminated, and where adverse events occur or are prevented.

Reflecting Beliefs about Injury Causation

Clear thinking about exposure and its role on injury causation helps leaders make breakthrough improvements in safety performance. Our firm invests significant resources helping to educate leaders in this area. We teach them to ask pointed questions to help others focus on the salient factors that contribute to any incident. It is critical that safety leaders recognize how the interaction of facilities and equipment, processes, and worker behavior may interact at the working interface to cause injuries. We also teach leaders to think more holistically about this subject of injury causation, extending their inquiries into the historical leadership and cultural factors that govern what occurs at the working interface. By doing so, these leaders have the best chance of identifying the factors that contribute to injuries and fatalities in their specific companies.

An organization that gives no thought to injury causation, in which injuries are seen as inevitable—just the cost of doing business—would be rated Unknown, the lowest stage in the Exposure discipline (Table 5–3). Organizations that have moved beyond blaming workers and have begun to recognize the role of behaviors and conditions in injury causation are at the intermediate Dualistic stage. Those that recognize even the most subtle influences on exposure and who consult employees during the design of processes, systems, and equipment are our heroes—at what we call the Expansive stage. They embody Values-driven safety.

TABLE 5–3. The Exposure Discipline.
How the organization thinks about injury causation.

	Facet	Defined as
AVOIDANCE	Unknown	The organization does not think about injury causation.
	Chaotic	Injuries are believed to be uncontrollable.
COMPLIANCE	Singular	Injuries are attributed solely to the actions of workers.
	Dualistic	Behaviors and conditions are recognized as having a role in injury causation.
VALUES	Holistic	The organization embraces a holistic view of behavioral reliability and recognizes multiple influences on exposure.
	Expansive	The organization recognizes even the most subtle and remote influences on exposure.

What you might see or hear

Injuries are seen as the cost of doing business and there is no formal attempt to control exposures. Here you will often see gross or repeated violations in compliance and regulatory conditions.

Leaders and employees alike might express the belief that "injuries are a part of the job." Safety measures will be driven by the need for compliance with regulatory requirements, rather any attempt to change outcomes. Injuries seem to "just happen" anyway.

Organizations at this stage recognize a relationship between people and accidents, but lack a sophisticated understanding of the configuration of people, systems, processes, and technology. Rudimentary "behavior-based" programs may be in place, but focus on changing behaviors (or framed around worker causation) can engender blame. Safety activities focus on training and other antecedents (e.g. posters, slogans). When that doesn't work, injury reports will advise involved employees to "be more careful."

At this stage, organizations recognize the role that behaviors and conditions play in injury causation. Safety efforts here expand to include a focus on improving conditions, such as the quality of PPE and working equipment. Behavior-based systems in these organizations start to become more reliable and collect data on the circumstances surrounding at-risk behaviors. Incident investigations are based on severity outcome.

Organizations at this stage have developed a more sophisticated taxonomy of exposure causation that recognizes multiple influences on exposure. Data from behavior-based systems will be used in conjunction with assessments of organizational systems and processes as they influence exposure. The depth of investigations here is based on the severity potential of the event, regardless of actual severity.

Organizations here recognize variation in severity potential represented by different types of exposures. Business decisions are weighed against their effect on exposure. For example, we know of organizations that consult employees in the design of new processes, systems, and equipment.

Evaluating the Exposure Discipline

At our client organizations we ask questions like these to assess the Exposure discipline. You can ask yourself these questions, too:

- When an accident occurs, how do your leaders describe what happened?

- What is the focus of investigations here?

- What determines the level of incident investigation—actual severity or potential severity?

- How wide is the net of safety reporting systems? Do the systems focus narrowly on behaviors or do they seek out multiple influences on safety?

- Is minimizing exposure applied to business decisions or is it simply applied to safety-focused activities?

- Are all accidents seen as preventable? Just some of them? None?

DEVELOPING THE FOUNDATIONAL DISCIPLINES

Our message for the senior-most leaders in organizations around the world is clear: Sharpening your understanding of the Foundational disciplines will help you build a healthy culture that supports the improvement of your safety performance. The following actions can set the stage:

1. Communicate a clear goal and compelling case for becoming a no-harm-to-anyone organization.

2. Learn more about the disciplines so that you can assess your organization's current level of functioning.

3. Coach and mentor others in the Foundational disciplines.

4. Assess your competency and your team's competency with regard to transformational leadership skills.

By becoming fluent in the Foundational disciplines, you will build a platform of understanding required to successfully influence the Safety and Organizational disciplines, which are described in the next two chapters.

CASE IN POINT: EXPOSURE

Fielding Risk at E.ON

E.ON is one of the world's largest investor-owned power and gas companies, generating electricity for UK homes and industry, and supplying gas to millions of people across the UK. Keeping the organization's field sales employees, known as Home Energy Consultants (HEC), safe can be particularly challenging. In addition to the hazards of door-to-door work—changing terrain, weather, and the odd dog—the role requires working predominantly alone with minimal supervision.

A rapid expansion in 2007 swelled HEC ranks from 30 to approximately 600 employees. While an exciting time for the company, the changes also took a toll on HECs. The attrition rate approached 200% and by March 2008, the Lost Time Incident Frequency Rate (LTIFR) had risen to 70. Initial interventions, such as a near hit reporting process and an accident hotline, helped cut the LTIFR nearly in half. However by 2009, the rate had stagnated. Analysis showed that the exposures were more complex than initially thought; HEC employees were 25 times more likely to be injured than E.ON meter readers, despite working in nearly identical conditions. The only difference was that these groups worked in different parts of the business.

The E.ON UK Centre Safety senior team partnered with the retail business to implement a behavior-based intervention that would identify and remove the unique exposures faced by HECs. Named GASS for Generating All Sales Safely, the team undertook observations based on a rigorously defined list of critical behaviors. The company also expanded its focus to cultural and leadership influences on exposure. Data that GASS team members collected was used both to remove barriers to safe work as well as provide leading indicators and a coaching strategy for leaders. The combination of a bottom-up input from employees and managed-down approach from leaders enabled HEC's to be closely involved and own the process while providing managers with appropriate skills to be able to develop and protect their teams.

By 2011, the GASS team had logged over 7,000 observations. The LTIFR was down to 10:11 and attrition was at an industry-low 85%. The approach has also reduced customer decay (those leaving E.ON) by 8% and has played a significant part in increasing per-HEC sales, representing an additional £25 million pounds per year.

NOTES

THE
SAFETY
DISCIPLINES

by Jim Spigener

THE SAFETY DISCIPLINES

In September 1998, two workers were killed and eight were injured in an explosion at Esso's natural gas plant in Longford, Australia. The explosion also disrupted the gas supply to some five million customers for two weeks. The event was started by a brittle fracture in a heat exchanger in the site's Gas Plant 1. Normally operating at a temperature of 100°C (212°F), the pump that regulated the flow of lean oil, which heated the exchanger, had stopped working for several hours. During that time condensate continued to flow through the exchanger, dropping the vessel's temperature to as low as -48°C (-54°F). When the pump was restarted, lean oil rushed back in at a scorching 230°C (446°F), causing the stress and resulting in a vapor cloud that was ignited shortly afterward. The fire burned for two days.[1]

The Royal Commission investigating the accident found a number of failures in the safety systems of the site. Among the most notable were the transfer of the engineers who had overseen safety operations to Melbourne, more than two hours away. The operators who remained had taken on a greater role in running the plant, but lacked sufficient knowledge or training in operating procedures for hazardous processes, even to the extent that warning and alarm systems routinely went off, further desensitizing employees to possible hazards. Data that would have alerted management to the potential for a catastrophic event were either unevenly distributed or never collected. A HAZOP (HAZard and OPerability) analysis of the plant that would likely

1   Victoria. Longford Royal Commission. *The Esso Longford gas plant accident: report of the Longford Royal Commission.* Government Printer for the State of Victoria, Melbourne, 1999.

have identified the risk was never carried out, and the site's reporting system did not allow information about exposures to this type of event (including similar conditions that had occurred only a month earlier) to reach the appropriate people.

Ultimately, the Royal Commission concluded that the causes of the event "amounted to a failure to provide and maintain so far as practicable a working environment that was safe and without risks to health."

Safety performance is immediately a function of the processes and systems that control exposure to injury. The four Safety disciplines drive safety functioning:

- **Structure** refers to the formal framework that supports safety decision making, accountability, and action. A robust governance structure—and the rigor and constancy it provides—is a hallmark of organizations with Zero Index safety performance.

- **Expertise** refers to the position, function, and contribution of the safety professional. This discipline is indicative of safety's status on the organizational agenda. It determines depth of safety expertise available and is a variable in how well safety drives others performance areas.

- **Scorecard** refers to the way in which the organization seeks and processes information about safety. The state of safety measurement affects the quality of safety management and is a source of natural antecedents and consequences that shape the culture. In higher performing organizations, this discipline extends beyond the traditional injury metrics that all organizations use today.

- **Safety-Enabling Systems** are the specific mechanisms used to manage and improve safety. This discipline is responsible for ensuring that people have the skills, competence, knowledge, processes, and procedures they need to work safely. The systems that enable the organization to execute in a way that manages exposure and risk have to not only be the right ones but also must be implemented in a way that truly captures the attention of all employees at all levels in the organization and addresses existing exposures.

At first, these disciplines seem relatively straightforward, but they can be deceptively complex to master. For instance, the configuration of an organization's metrics—part of the Scorecard discipline—can mask the true level of exposure in the workplace. The frequency of safety meetings and trainings—an aspect of an organization's Safety-Enabling Systems—doesn't necessarily correlate to actual skill levels or reductions in exposure. The existence of a safety decision-making framework—part of the Structure discipline—doesn't protect safety from continual conflicts with other business processes and initiatives. Regardless of the industry, under performance in the four Safety disciplines is the surest direct path to injuries. Let's take a look at each one.

THE STRUCTURE DISCIPLINE

As an organization sets out to achieve a goal, it naturally begins to define roles, responsibilities, and lines of accountability. Structure, sometimes called governance or management, defines how the goal will be met and is the formal means for supporting decision making, accountability, and action.

Structure matters to safety in particular because it connects the stated goals of the organization to execution. Creating an organization in which "Safety is who we are" requires people who define the organization (chiefly leaders, but also others who influence what happens and how) to be involved in the line-of-sight governance of safety execution. The more inclusive a structure is of all the roles and levels that influence safety activities, the more effective the governance will be at driving consistent outcomes.

Safety structure is far upstream of outcomes, which means a flawed system can go undetected, sometimes for years.

Providing the Framework for Safety Execution

The structure of safety determines ultimately how, or whether, outcomes are achieved. Effective governance enables the organization and its leaders to influence safety in a very meaningful and powerful way. It can also create a strong personal connection between employees and the organization and its leaders—a connection pivotal to improving behavioral reliability in today's flatter, leaner organizations, where employees have more latitude and less oversight than ever before.

Structure is also the discipline that trips up many organizations before they even get started. Safety structure is far upstream of safety outcomes, which means that a flawed system for managing accountabilities and decision making can go undetected, sometimes for years.

Recently, we worked with an oil company that was struggling with a long-running plateau. Although the activities and practices they were using were sound, we discovered that they had trouble allocating resources needed for many safety activities. Digging into the issue, we came to find out that there was a parallel cost-containment effort driven by the organization's finance department. Yet none of the financial personnel were aligned within the safety governance structure. As a result, safety needs were frequently trumped by the drive to contain costs.

Achieving Zero Index performance requires that every person in the organization understands what their roles are and what behaviors fulfill those roles. How those parameters are defined is illustrated in the various stages of this discipline (Table 6–1). Rudimentary governance structures tend to favor a single person or group having ownership of safety, whereas more effective organizations include topmost leaders, safety professionals, and even non-safety functions in the oversight of safety activities.

NOTES

TABLE 6–1. The Structure Discipline.
The formal structure that supports safety decision making, accountability, and action.

	Facet	Defined as
AVOIDANCE	Vacant	Safety is not formally owned by anyone.
AVOIDANCE	Orphaned	Oversight for safety is held solely within an individual person.
COMPLIANCE	Relegated	Goal-setting and oversight is assigned solely to a department or function.
COMPLIANCE	Supported	Goal setting and oversight is supported by senior safety leaders.
VALUES	Sponsored	Senior operations leadership sponsors and oversees safety in conjunction with senior safety professionals.
VALUES	Integrated	Executive management, board members, senior leaders, and safety professionals work together to sponsor safety in a highly effective way.

What you might see or hear

There is no formal structure for safety oversight. This stage is typically characterized by an "every man for himself" mindset. Safety decisions are made only when there is a clear need or a serious problem. Safety practices tend to be based on precedent (what was decided before) without consideration of current business realities.

Safety has a formal owner whose work is largely focused on basic requirements. Safety performance is generally isolated from other organizational activities. Lacking broad oversight, individual supervisors or managers will tend to make safety decisions at their own discretion, with high degrees of variability in quality and results.

Safety decision making and direction is limited to the members of the department or function with formal ownership of it. Decision making is done in small groups, typically at the site level, and isolated from corporate initiatives. Safety activities here often compete with other initiatives and business needs for resources.

Safety tends to be recognized formally at the corporate level and has a designated sponsor there. Safety roles and responsibilities are defined for levels throughout the organization. Safety needs begin to hold equal weight with other business needs as the organization recognizes the business benefits of safety.

The rationale for safety activities is expressed in terms of the business's wider objectives, rather than just the business benefits. Safety has "a seat at the table" in senior leadership discussions. Operational leaders throughout the organization have a defined role in safety.

Safe work is treated as synonymous with good performance. Operational and senior leaders participate in safety decision making, planning, and action and routinely weigh the impact of their decisions on safety. Safety has a formal and visible presence in the organization's highest objectives and holds a significant position on the Board's agenda.

Evaluating the Structure Discipline

To assess your organization's performance with respect to safety governance, or structure, ask yourself:

- Who owns safety in the organization? Who needs to own safety here?

- Does the ownership include operational leaders? Senior leaders?

- How are safety goals defined for employees at different levels? What do the goals focus on?

- Who reviews safety data and reports?

- Is the decision-making process related to safety clear? Unclear?

- How does the ownership of safety manifest itself at different levels? If you asked people in the field what triggers the halting of a job for safety reasons, what would they say?

- How do safety decision making and action integrate with other business initiatives and processes?

CASE IN POINT: STRUCTURE

Mapping Out Safety at ExxonMobil

In 2006, ExxonMobil walked away from what would have been the world's deepest offshore well in the Gulf of Mexico's Blackbeard West formation. The company had already invested $180 million and drilled 30,000 of the planned 32,000 feet below the seabed. Despite the advanced stage of the project, company engineers deemed the well too risky to proceed any further.

Abandoning the project provoked harsh criticism from industry analysts. Some said the company "lacked the guts" to finish the well and was too risk averse. Despite the flak, ExxonMobil executives stood firm. Four year later, the decision would prove downright prescient. The Deepwater Horizon, a similar project in many ways to Blackbeard West, would end up costing rival BP billions of dollars in clean up costs alone. In Congressional testimony shortly following the Deepwater disaster, Exxon chief executive Rex Tillerson explained the difference between the two outcomes simply: "We would not have drilled the well they did."

The decision to abandon the Blackbeard West well was a result of ExxonMobil's Operations Integrity Management System (OIMS). And it was just the kind of thing OIMS was designed for. Initially developed following the 1989 Exxon Valdez disaster, OIMS is a safety framework made up of 11 distinct focus areas that measure and mitigate safety, security, health, and environmental risk at ExxonMobil. The organization uses OIMS as a roadmap for safety management and decisions as the 11 elements dictate everything from how risk is assessed and managed to how local business units handle relationships with the communities in which they operate.

The first OIMS element, management leadership, commitment, and accountability, is also considered the driver of all the other elements. This element defines both how management establishes safety policy and expectations as well as how leaders are to show visible commitment to safety.

SOURCES: Jad Mouawad, "New Culture of Caution at Exxon after Valdez," New York Times, July 12, 2010. Steve Levine, "Exxon: Juggernaut or Dinosaur?", BusinessWeek, February 5, 2009.www.exxonmobil.com/corporate/safety_ops_oims.

THE EXPERTISE DISCIPLINE

Whatever the area of expertise, whether as an industrial hygienist, safety engineer, loss prevention engineer, or any of a myriad of other titles, the safety professional's core duty is guiding the organization in the prevention of exposures that cause harm to people, property, and the environment. Traditionally, the safety professional has executed that role in a very limited way, serving as an administrator of safety programs—or even in some cases as the safety cop. As organizations come to recognize the strategic importance of safety performance, however, they are also beginning to rethink the unique role and potential of their safety experts. Safety professionals have the expertise to guide the organization's management of exposure and the execution of initiatives and activities. Could they not also lead the development of safety strategy, support change execution, and partner with leaders at the highest levels in advancing overall operational performance?

> What is your role in guiding your organization to safety?

The answer to this question is largely one of education and perception. In most cases, the safety professional was never trained to be a change agent and the organization has typically pigeonholed safety expertise within a narrow sphere. Repositioning the safety professional's role requires both the development of safety personnel and a realignment of expectations within the organization itself. Safety professionals must develop fluency in change management methodology, the role of behavior in performance, culture, and leadership. At the same time, organizations need to advance their understanding of the role of safety in the overall strategy of the organization, and redefine the scope of the safety professional's responsibilities and reach.

Reflecting the Role of the Safety Professional

In our experience, the position, function, and contribution of the safety professional correlate with the sophistication of safety strategy and execution. When safety professionals are limited to the enforcement of rules or the running of programs, the expertise available to the leaders who drive the strategy and operation of the organization is similarly limited. On the other hand, when organizations engage safety professionals as partners in change, they necessarily create access to safety and performance expertise at the highest levels in a way that supports operational excellence (Table 6–2).

NOTES

TABLE 6–2. The Expertise Discipline.
The position, function, and contribution of the safety professional.

	Facet	Defined as
AVOIDANCE	Absent	There is no safety professional.
	Enforcer	The safety professional enforces rules in an effort to reduce liability and cost associated with incidents.
COMPLIANCE	Administrator	The safety professional administers traditional safety activities and responds to safety issues.
	Facilitator	The safety professional is guiding the safety process and is often the main driver of it.
VALUES	Agent	The safety professional is a change agent and works with senior leadership on direction and execution.
	Partner	The safety professional is a strategic partner to leaders at all levels in achieving the highest standards of performance.

What you might see or hear

Safety expertise is not recognized as important and there is no formal role defined for a safety professional. Individual managers deal with safety issues as they arise, with significant variability in results.

The safety professional is seen as the "safety cop". Safety learning is generally limited to the individual safety professional who is consulted only when there is a problem. Safety professionals are hired and evaluated based on regulatory expertise.

The safety professional tends to be a "fixer" who is consulted for addressing and resolving basic safety issues. Safety professionals are hired and evaluated based on regulatory and administrative expertise.

The organization relies on the safety professional for implementing safety processes and activities. Leaders look to the safety professional for information on safety performance within traditional parameters. The safety professional spends a significant portion of time creating programs and training workers. Safety professionals are hired and evaluated based on technical expertise.

The highest ranking safety professional is a resource to operational leaders, guiding safety activities. The professional focuses on assessing current performance and making recommendations. The safety professional is hired and evaluated based on technical and business expertise. At this level, the safety professional spends a greater portion of time advising leaders.

At this stage, the safety leadership role is used to develop high-potential employees and the safety professional is hired and evaluated on business and strategy expertise. The lead safety professional spends a large portion of her time working with senior management on performance issues.

Evaluating the Expertise Discipline

To understand how the role of safety professional is developed and deployed in your organization, ask yourself:

- How do we describe the role of safety professionals here?

- What criteria do we use to hire and evaluate safety professionals?

- How do safety professionals spend their time? For example, what percentage of time do they spend on enforcement compared with consulting with operational or senior leaders?

- What is the highest level held by a safety professional in our organization?

- How do we leverage the knowledge and expertise of safety professionals in our daily business decisions and activities?

- What is the career path for safety professionals here?

CASE IN POINT: EXPERTISE

From Police to Partner

Developing the Expertise discipline is sometimes as much about changing perceptions as it is about developing the role. In one company we worked with, safety professionals performed a traditional, technician role familiar to many organizations. The professionals collected data, compiled reports, and, frequently, acted as enforcers. Not surprisingly, their interaction with executives was limited to delivering reports using previously determined templates. When a new senior safety director met with the safety professionals, he was struck by how little of their insight and experience ever made its way up to where safety strategy was formed.

The new director set out to position safety professionals as consultants to executive leadership, rather than just technicians delivering information. The trick was to "up their game"; they needed a new model for what safety professionals were and could be. The director organized a series of training sessions using serious injuries, a major organizational concern, as a focal point. The objective was to help the safety professionals become comfortable with analyzing incident reports in a deep way and then developing their ability to collaborate with others on addressing their findings, specifically the high-potential exposures uncovered in their analysis.

Safety professionals in this organization now routinely pull together data analysis that separates exposures and near misses by severity potential (high, mid, low) and present their findings to executives personally in addition to delivering reports by email. The result is that safety professionals and executives are having a much different discussion than they did previously. Safety experts (as they are now known) point out areas of concern to executives, advise leaders on how best to apply resources based on potential, and provide an "on the ground" picture of safety functioning that executives wouldn't get otherwise. As the safety director put it, "We're applying safety expertise now to organizational learning instead of 'putting people in jail'."

THE SCORECARD DISCIPLINE

Unlike most other business measures—think earnings growth or debt load—the traditional measures of safety performance tell us little about where existing functioning actually is, and where it is headed. The deficiency of safety measurement in describing actual performance is so common as to be a cliché: many catastrophic industrial events occur in organizations with a history of low injury rates (and who may have even been recognized previously for "high" safety performance). The reality is that there are many variables that determine the quality of safety functioning. It is often only after a serious event that a picture of these elements (e.g., the execution of safety systems, the consistency of follow through on safety issues, the quality of culture and leadership) begin to paint a truer picture of the safety functioning present before the incident—one that could have been detected with the right set of metrics, processes, and analysis.

The Scorecard discipline describes how well the organization seeks and processes essential indicators of safety performance. This discipline is measured both in terms of the comprehensiveness of the set of measures the organization uses, as well as the way in which the organization collects, processes, and interprets that information. The higher an organization functions in the Scorecard discipline, the more effectively it is able to manage safety performance and the better leaders can steer the culture by providing antecedents and consequences that match desired activities.

What We Measure

The first concern of the Scorecard discipline is determining an appropriate mix of measures. Zero Index performance requires indicators that tell us where we are and where we are headed. It also requires measures that allow the organization to detect changes, and responses to changes, with precision. Experience has shown us that there is no perfect suite of measures common to all organizations. Instead, high-performing organizations aim for a set of measures that provide useful and robust indicators of how they are doing against their unique objectives and appropriate to the application and level of the organization. The suite of measures useful at the executive level (where the question "how are we doing" is often the focus) necessarily differs from the measures that are useful at the mid-levels of an organization (where the question, "What are we going to do in order to improve?" should be the focus). Fundamentally, any mix includes both leading and lagging indicators.

Lagging Indicators

As the standard measures of safety, lagging indicators offer the advantage of helping organizations benchmark their performance against industry. Lagging indicators, such as Lost Work Case rate, Total Recordable or Medical Case rate (OSHA recordable rate in the United States), serve as the report card at the end of the day and tell us in broad terms whether our efforts are on the right track. At the same time, lagging indicators have significant limitations for steering safety performance. Many lagging indicators used today are driven by government regulations and financial concerns and by themselves have a tremendous amount of noise in them. What looks like a very good OSHA recordable rate on paper can mask a high level of risks that have simply not been realized. Lagging indicators also introduce a delay in evaluating performance. They don't accurately tell you how the organization is performing in real time and they have a diminishing value as they decrease. The more an organization improves, the greater its need for upstream predictive metrics and a more sophisticated evaluation and action protocol.

Leading Indicators

In addition to measuring lagging indicators, high-performance organizations typically measure leading indicators, upstream measures that predict the outcome of interest (as opposed to merely occurring before the outcome of interest). The best leading indicators have two features that set them apart:

The best leading indicators are both predictive and diagnostic. 1) They have a robust research base establishing their predictive relationship to an outcome of interest, and 2) they provide diagnostic information about how to improve the outcome of interest. In our consultations with clients, we evaluate the organization's employment (or lack thereof) of these leading indicators:

Exposure. Excellence in safety is directly related to how effectively the exposure to hazards is controlled throughout the organization. Organizations need to measure the levels of exposure to hazards, and changes within those levels, across the business.

Safety activities. Organizations need actionable information on the quality and scope of those activities responsible for driving safety performance. Specific activities will vary across the organization and are not limited to traditional safety programs. Measured activities may specifically include the "critical few" rules or procedures that most directly influence high-severity potential situations, such as lock-out/tag-out or requiring people to tie off when working at heights. They may also include organizational practices that have a profound impact on safety, such as employee selection criteria, performance management, and decision making at all levels.

Climate and culture. The factors that correlate with high performance in safety are well established and easy to measure.[2] Having a good baseline of the culture and climate characteristics linked to safety outcomes allows the organization to target resources in the right areas (for example, on teamwork or on procedural justice) and periodically assess progress. Effective measures of culture and climate also allow the organization to create a concrete, compelling case for asking people to put their shoulders to the wagon in order to effect real organizational change.

Leadership. In our experience, the leadership-culture connection cannot be separated. Research has identified specific leadership practices[3] that predict and drive safety excellence. Whereas some leadership practices are fairly obvious, in most cases leaders are flying blind when it comes to knowing how well they are executing these practices and how they are being perceived by those around

A lack of knowledge about your leadership behavior is a game stopper.

them in the organization. Not knowing your effectiveness as a leader leads to unacceptable variation in performance-driving behavior, a loss of consistency in the message the organization receives, and, worse, a pessimistic and cynical culture. A lack of knowledge about your leadership behavior is a game stopper if you are serious about achieving Zero Index performance. A good measure of leadership behavior should provide organizations with a diagnostic capability to detect and address variations that can undermine safety efforts. If we get the leadership behavior right, we get a high-performing culture; if we get the culture right, we get excellence and sustainability. This is too important to leave to guesswork.

Before we leave the discussion about leading indicators, it is important to note that not all upstream measures are valid leading indicators. The presence in and of itself of an upstream measure (or suite of measures) is not sufficient to monitor and manage safety performance. Too often in the safety field, organizations measure activities such as hours spent in safety training without measuring whether those increased hours actually paid off in better safety performance.

---

2   Thomas R. Krause, *Leading with Safety*, (Hoboken: Wiley Interscience, 2005).

3   Discussed further in Chapter 7.

How We Use the Data

Ultimately, the power of measurement comes down to how the organization processes and applies the information it gathers. Data use poses several problems. For many organizations the problem is not that they don't have enough to measure, it's knowing how to process the various indicators that they do have, particularly if they are tracking a comprehensive mix of leading and lagging indicators. In organizations that focus on injuries and meeting certain numbers, safety metrics can become tainted by the emotional significance of certain indicators as they experience natural fluctuations. How leaders respond to data, particularly if it includes bad news, can make people reluctant to provide complete and timely information and compromise the integrity of the inputs into the system.

High-functioning organizations use practices that help them quickly navigate the macro and micro views of safety functioning without getting bogged down in the noise. They also focus on establishing reliability in measurement activities and remove negative consequences for reporting or using data. For example, many organizations establish rules around what data require further analysis, they give leaders a grounding in statistical methods and variation, and they set expectations around the tone and consistency of follow-through.

The stages of the Scorecard discipline are shown in Table 6–3.

TABLE 6–3. The Scorecard Discipline.
How the organization seeks and uses information about safety.

	Facet	Defined as
AVOIDANCE	Limited	Accident data are tracked to the extent required by regulation, but are not reported internally.
	Stunted	Accident data are reported internally but are not regularly reviewed or used by management.
COMPLIANCE	Cyclical	Management tracks lagging indicators and reacts when the numbers rise. Most consequences that result from the data are negative.
	Consistent	Management tracks lagging indicators and responds to rises and falls with a steady focus on improvement. Positive and negative consequences for performance result from their use.
VALUES	Dynamic	Management tracks leading and lagging indicators, with a focus on valid diagnostic information that can be used to improve the outcomes. Data are used to remove barriers, improve systems, and enable people to work safely.
	Enterprise	Management expands leading indicators to include leadership and organizational influences on exposure. Response to the information reinforces critical safety behaviors for people at every level and in every function.

What you might see or hear

Required tracking data are available with varying levels of completeness, however they are not used or reported within the business. Injury reporting tends not to be consistent or reliable.

Accident data are formally circulated internally, however they are seldom used for improvement activities. Managers may not know how to interpret or apply the information. Minor injuries and near misses may not be reported.

Management has more engagement with accident data at this stage, however data use tends to be reactive. Reporting injuries will sometimes cause problems for employees and their supervisors. Exposures are often addressed only after they are implicated in an event. Periods of low or no injuries are seen as evidence of high safety performance.

Organizations at this stage have a laser focus on lagging metrics (injury rates, lost times, etc.) and apply steady pressure on improving the rates. Reporting injuries and near misses generally does not cause problems for employees and their supervisors.

Leaders approach the data within metrics as a learning opportunity. Managers and supervisors are trained to interpret and respond to safety data constructively. People feel comfortable personally reporting their own injuries and near misses. Metrics grow in scope and sophistication as leaders seek more indicative data. One organization we work with is expanding its tracking to include "total hurts" with an objective of fostering a reporting culture.

At this stage, injury data is typically too sparse to be of significant use in analysis. Organizations here use a sophisticated sampling strategy that approaches data as an indicator of operational functioning. Metrics are a major object of study, review, deliberation, and reconsideration as leaders and safety professionals look for evidence of the next event.

Evaluating the Scorecard Discipline

Assessing the Scorecard discipline requires attention to what we're measuring, how we are measuring it, and the way we use and respond to data. Ask yourself, for example:

- What data are we tracking? What is the mix of leading to lagging indicators?

- What predictive data do we track?

- If someone asked us to paint a picture of the exposure to hazard as it is today in organization, would we have the data to tell them?

- How do we collect information? Are there negative consequences to accurate reporting?

- How do we use the information we collect? Do we report it internally? Use it for decision making? Do we respond to exposure information consistently?

- How do we process information? What are the rules for what to dig into?

- How reliable are our tracking activities perceived to be?

CASE IN POINT: SCORECARD

Upgrading a Dashboard

One organization we worked with used the same safety dashboard for many years. Each month, a safety committee composed of senior operations managers and safety professionals met to review and discuss their lengthy dashboard. Section 1 showed OSHA recordable incident rates from each of their locations, lost workday incident rates, and a breakdown of injuries by body part. Section 2 listed Tier 1, 2, and 3 process safety events. Section 3 listed the status of action items, recommendations, open issues, and past due inspections. Publicly, many senior leaders joked about the length of the report. Privately, a few leaders admitted that safety meetings were a waste of time, particularly the dashboard review. Discussions during the review focused on whether or not the numbers were accurate. Managers who had not had incidents that month said nothing, while managers who had incidents in their areas argued with the safety professionals about incident management, classification, and record-keeping. Discussion of the action items, recommendations, and open issues were limited except immediately before or after an inspection.

The organization's senior safety leader asked us to help develop a new safety dashboard. The goal was to present a set of information that would prompt a productive and proactive safety discussion. Senior leaders needed to be able to quickly assess the state of safety functioning but also have enough detail to respond with precise, and upstream, action. As the leader put it, "I don't need to know how many body parts were injured... we can all count. I need management to be able focus on reducing exposure to the most serious incidents in their areas."

Working with members of the safety committee, we developed a hierarchical report. Functionally, the dashboard offered a high-level view of a mix of critical indicators. Leaders were able drill down for additional detail as they needed. Substantively, we balanced traditional measures with new leading indicators. Exposure metrics tracked levels of exposure to both personal and process safety hazards. Control metrics looked at indicators of functioning in both safety systems and the management systems that supported them, for example the proportion of safety audit findings resolved within 60 days (personal safety) or on-time completion of critical safety equipment testing (process safety).

Right away, leaders were surprised by the level of detail available upstream of a crisis. The report was both easier to read and more detailed. Most important, the new dashboard has allowed the senior leadership team to develop a better fluency with the moving parts of safety in their organization.

THE SAFETY-ENABLING SYSTEMS DISCIPLINE

Safety-Enabling Systems, the last of the four Safety disciplines, are the specific mechanisms used to manage and improve safety. Used well, they ensure that people have the skills, competence, knowledge, processes, and procedures to work safely. The list of activities that make up Safety-Enabling Systems varies little across most industries. For example, almost all companies do a risk assessment on processes and equipment, conduct safety trainings, hold safety meetings, write procedures, etc. The real difference is not the list but in the effectiveness of these systems—how they are executed and how the organization uses them. Here, the variation is huge—and so are the results.

A few years ago, two companies in the same industry approached us for help in improving their safety performance. One organization had a lost-time injury frequency of 0.09 and an OSHA recordable rate[4] of a bit under 1.0. The other had a lost-time frequency of 0.90 and an OSHA recordable rate of about 7.0. Despite the wide gulf in performance, their practices, at least on the surface, looked a great deal alike.

As part of an assessment, we conducted interviews with supervisors from each company. When asked if they held safety meetings, the teams from both companies enthusiastically replied that they did. Each team described very similar activities; both had large monthly group meetings, weekly team or crew meetings, and daily toolbox huddles. Then we asked each group why they did these meetings. In the poor-performing company, the supervisors unanimously responded that they held safety meetings because they were "told to". It was just part of the job. In the higher-performing company, supervisors gave a range of answers. They held meetings because it helped them understand safety, collaborate on difficult issues, listen to the barriers that employees faced, and display leadership and concern for people's safety. For these supervisors, safety meetings were not a checkbox to be ticked. The meetings were part of a bigger picture.

What is the breadth and effectiveness of your current Safety-Enabling Systems?

The quality of execution was evident in how the meetings themselves were conducted. In the poor-performing company, five of the six meetings we sat in on consisted of popping in a video and turning out the lights. Many of the supervisors did not know how to conduct an effective safety meeting

---

4   Lost-time injury rate in the United States is calculated as the number of injuries requiring days away from work per 100 full-time employees. OSHA rate refers to the number of all recordable workplace injuries per 100 full-time employees.

and were solely concerned with making sure everyone signed the roster. Attendance, not quality, was the measure of success. Not surprisingly, these meetings were not very effective in lowering exposure or enabling people to identify and deal with the risks that they encountered on a daily basis. To employees, the message was that safety is something that we give lip service to but are not actually committed to. More implicitly, the message was: "You guys should feel free to do whatever you think is OK."

As organizations move toward Zero Index performance, the development of Safety-Enabling Systems typically progresses in breadth (are activities focused on risk or just on compliance?) and execution (how effective are these activities or are we simply checking off the box?). An excellent indicator of the development of the Safety-Enabling Systems discipline is the quality of behavior-based safety processes, if they are used. Understood, built, and executed properly, these systems are very effective at moving the organization from an injury focus to an exposure-reduction focus. Yet, like other systems and tools used in this discipline, emphasis determines the quality and outcome. At the lower levels of functioning, behavior-based safety tends to be a mind-numbing, box-checking, cover-your-behind sort of exercise, done to satisfy a requirement. As organizations advance in this discipline and they pay more attention to the principles of continuous improvement, employee engagement, and system improvement overall, they find that their behavior-based safety systems create a profoundly positive impact on the organization's culture, level of exposure, and safety performance.

The Engine of Risk Management

To develop the Safety-Enabling Systems discipline, the systems and tools must be in place to enable safe work, with the professionals leading these systems optimizing the systems' effect. The full range of this discipline is shown in Table 6–4.

TABLE 6–4. The Safety-Enabling Systems Discipline.
The specific mechanisms used to manage and improve safety.

	Facet	Defined as
AVOIDANCE	Sparse	Few, if any, safety-enabling systems are in place.
	Inconsistent	Safety-enabling systems are rules-based and inconsistently used.
COMPLIANCE	Compliant	Rules-based safety-enabling systems are consistently used. Systems that dig into root causes begin to emerge.
	Advanced	Safety-enabling systems are risk-based but inconsistently used.
VALUES	Reliable	Risk-based safety-enabling systems are consistently used.
	Futuristic	Highly reliable safety-enabling systems anticipate and prepare for future risks.

What you might see or hear

At this level, there are few formal systems for supporting safe work. Safety rules tend to be developed on an ad hoc basis and typically only in response to a crisis.

At this stage, systems are heavily weighted toward rules and compliance rather than exposure identification or reduction. There tends to be high variability in the understanding and enforcement of basic policies and procedures. When rules occasionally are enforced, employees may feel unfairly singled out. Skills development is sporadic and training may be over generalized or irrelevant to the work.

Employees and management are essentially aligned in their understanding and use of basic policies and procedures. Safety meetings or other activities are routine but may tend to be done out of rote. Required PPE and administrative controls are consistently used. At the same time, some work teams and their managers may not have the skills and knowledge they need to enable safe work in all situations or to communicate effectively about safety. Rudimentary root cause analysis is present in some areas.

There is a formal process for near miss reporting and tracking. Hazard identification systems look for exposures with varying effectiveness. Risk-based policies, procedures, and rules can vary in their use, leading some employees to feel that following them is "optional". Atypical exposures may go undetected until an event occurs.

Hazard recognition systems engage employees, supervisors, managers and contractors in identifying and mitigating risks. Risk-based policies, procedures, and rules are applied consistently. Work teams and their managers have the skills and knowledge they need to enable safe work and communicate effectively and credibly about safety. Exposure identification and resolution is consistent and reliable.

Exposure identification systems adapt with the business and routinely identify risks as the configurations change. Work teams and their managers are fluent in exposure identification and handle atypical tasks as safely as routine work.

Evaluating the Safety-Enabling Systems Discipline

Assessing the Safety-Enabling Systems discipline is about understanding the systems' connection to, and support of, the organization's safety objectives. Ask yourself:

- What safety systems do we have in place?

- What is the basis for choosing the systems that we have? Do we select them based on regulatory requirements alone or on risk assessment?

- How are these systems actually being executed? Do people use them in a way that enables a constant downward pressure on exposure?

- What systems do we have in place for addressing exposures with a high potential of causing life-altering injuries?

CASE IN POINT: SAFETY-ENABLING SYSTEMS

Calibrating Safety Systems in Amtrak's Mechanical Department

Keeping Amtrak's nation-wide equipment safe and reliable is in large part the responsibility of the organization's mechanical department. Made up of 4,500 dedicated employees across the United States working predominantly within a dozen major terminal locations, the mechanical department cleans, inspects, maintains, and dispatches long and short distance trains for their next assignments, often in the very same day. In addition, three main shop facilities are dedicated to perform component repair and major overhaul work, which periodically involve stripping down and upgrading cars from the ground up.

With the primary focus placed on equipment performance, there can be lost opportunities for safety system improvements. Maintaining consistent performance standards, let alone implementing a culture of continuous improvement, across a group spread over thousands of miles is a significant challenge. While the work and exposures are similar, sites tended to develop solutions to common problems in isolation.

In 2006, the mechanical department implemented Process Focus Teams (or PFTs) to capture and share best practices across all disciplines of work. The Safety PFT, led by process owner Tommy Farr, specifically takes innovation and insight around safety-enabling systems from the individual site to the national level with a heavy emphasis on an open and collaborative approach. The team is made up of 20 employees who represent every division in the country. Team members visit sites to document standards of excellence in safety systems and routinely develop and distribute best practices with photos and articles that best represent their findings.

One of the Safety PFT's successes is a program called *Another Set of Eyes*. Under this initiative, a subset of the Safety PFT visits facilities to observe a site's working environment from a fresh perspective. Bringing in Another Set of Eyes helps prevent the "wallpaper" effect that many get when they work in the same place for years, and exposures are less visible and more likely to become unnoticed. The program involves a walkabout and performing observations of the work environment, such as housekeeping, infrastructure, condition of tools, as well as how mechanics interact with equipment. The team members then provide the site leadership team with informal feedback on what they're doing well, what they could improve upon, and leave them with lean management tools to aid with the improvement efforts.

Another Set of Eyes represents an effective complement of the Mechanical Department's safety program in its goal to reduce risk exposures and provide all employees a safe work environment.

ADVANCING THE SAFETY DISCIPLINES

Getting safety right requires highly functioning systems that work together in mitigating exposure to injury. Although leaders need to optimize each of the Safety disciplines individually, they must also work to ensure that the disciplines are configured to inform, support, and enable high functioning in all the others. To improve performance in the four Safety disciplines, ask yourself:

- What is the net effect of the Safety disciplines together? How well do they realize the organization's vision and objectives?

- What is the organization's current level of functioning in each of the disciplines?

- How does each discipline currently affect the functioning of the others? For example, how does the way we measure safety (the Scorecard discipline) influence the way we execute safety systems (the Safety-Enabling Systems discipline)?

- What is the relationship between the Safety disciplines in this chapter and the Foundational disciplines covered earlier, in chapter 5? How does our current functioning in Vision, Engagement, and Exposure shape how we execute the Safety disciplines?

- What factors are keeping our performance where it is today? What would we need to change to move forward?

The Safety disciplines are at the heart of safety performance improvement, yet for an organization to develop safety as a strategic activity—indeed, to move safety performance itself forward—its leaders need to understand the connections between safety activities and practices and the rest of the business. In the next chapter, we discuss the three Organizational disciplines, Leadership, Culture, and Sustaining Systems, which are critical to driving and sustaining safety functioning.

NOTES

NOTES

THE ORGANIZATIONAL DISCIPLINES

by Sarah K. Smith

THE ORGANIZATIONAL DISCIPLINES

On a summer evening in 1988, a blast ripped through the gas compression module on the North Sea offshore oil platform Piper Alpha. Within two hours, the platform was engulfed in flames. Within three, the entire structure had collapsed into the sea, taking with it the lives of 167 men and causing a total insured loss of more than $3 billion.

The immediate cause of the fire was a failure of the permit-to-work system. Operators had activated a condensate pump not knowing that it had been taken offline for repair in the previous shift—or that in place of the pump's pressure safety valve was a loosely fitted blind flange. Subsequent failures in other systems, such as platform design (e.g., firewalls that were never made blast-proof when the platform was converted from oil to gas production), decision making (the platform manager reportedly panicked and did not order evacuations or direct the waiting fire boats into action), and the inoperability of firefighting equipment and some life rafts, compounded the initial error into a crisis of catastrophic proportions.

Subsequent investigation found a cascade of mistakes and decisions related to multiple factors, including the design of the platform, production and expansion decisions, personnel management, and inspection and maintenance issues. In other words, the chain of events did not begin with a single person's mistake. It reached all the way back to the operating company's processes and leadership, and even to the regulatory agencies overseeing oil production in the region.

It is often said that safety happens in moments. Sometimes a serious injury results from a single decision or action that set in motion a fateful chain of events. More often than not, safety outcomes are driven by a steady succession of organizational decisions and actions that shape the moment to moment execution of safety objectives. Systems and processes reinforce certain ways of doing things and discourage others. Shared norms of behavior dictate how (or whether) safety requirements are met. What employees perceive as leadership priorities influence what gets attention, and what gets neglected, in day-to-day operations.

Root cause analyses of incidents show clearly that al-though an individual can be blamed, the real cause of any incident is almost always a failure of organizational systems. Yes, if the operator had taken the time to alert the oncoming shift to the status of critical equipment, the incident might have been avoided. But if the systems don't provide for adequate training—if shortcuts are common-

> **How prevalent is blame in your organization?**

place and seen daily by supervisors or by any leader who bothers to look, if relations among departments and individuals are tense and strained—then it is profoundly unjust to look backward after an incident that was predictable, given the systems and cultural factors, and blame the employee.

Ensuring the effectiveness of safety execution is a function of the Organizational disciplines: Leadership, Culture, and Sustaining Systems. These disciplines can best be described as the core—or solar plexus—of the organization. Through them, organizations create, strengthen, and support performance.

Culture refers to the values, beliefs, and unstated assumptions that influence what people do and the way they do it. Culture can create the optimal conditions for effective management, leadership, and safe productive work—or it can undermine them.

Leadership describes how all leaders are developed and deployed in safety. Leadership influences the culture characteristics predictive of safety outcomes and determines the strength and longevity of safety systems.

Finally, the **Sustaining Systems** discipline refers to the organizational antecedents and consequences that support effective safety management, leadership, and performance. In essence, Sustaining Systems systematically influence the motivation to work safely.

Individually and in combination, these disciplines drive all activities related to safety performance improvement and directly influence the probability that those activities will be successful. As with the disciplines outlined in previous chapters, the Organizational disciplines also exist on a continuum. Understanding how these three disciplines evolve over time and what they look like at each stage is useful for diagnosing the state of safety and will help leaders understand how the system of safety works.

THE CULTURE DISCIPLINE

Every workplace has a discernible "way" that things are done. If you watch carefully and long enough how people make decisions and approach tasks, you can learn what the people in that organization value and uncover

Organizational culture simply refers to the shared, often unconscious values, attitudes, standards, and assumptions that govern behavior.

the unwritten rules of the workplace. Organizational culture simply refers to the shared, often unconscious values, attitudes, standards, and assumptions that govern behavior. Culture shapes how people navigate the organization, especially in situations that lack clearly defined rules and procedures. It influences how people interpret directives and initiatives, how people interact, and even how long people choose to stay.

Although a culture is always present in a peripheral way, understanding exactly how the culture is influencing performance can be frustratingly difficult. After all, what exactly defines culture? What does it look like? And how exactly does it influence performance? The Culture discipline is about understanding the collective effect of these attitudes, beliefs, and assumptions with respect to safety actions at every level. There is a body of literature that identifies dimensions of organizational culture predictive of safety outcomes, and in a diagnostic scenario these would be viewed in great detail. For the purpose of examining the whole system, we describe it here in simpler terms: how the culture develops as a reflection of the value for safety.

Why Culture Matters

For business leaders, understanding the connection between culture and safety requires understanding several key principles:

Culture reflects organizational relationships. Among the most powerful predictors of safe outcomes are the cultural artifacts of the relationships employees have with their superiors and with the organization as a whole. Several of these factors can be understood from social exchange theory, which says that important aspects of relationships (between individuals, or between an individual and a group) can be viewed as a series of exchanges. For example, employees treated with respect and offered support by their supervisors are more likely to reciprocate through job performance, extra-role behavior, and loyalty. On the other hand, employees who feel demeaned or disrespected are more likely to disengage.

Culture determines how people engage the work. Up close, culture shapes how people respond to different situations. For example, in a culture that values speaking up, employees are more likely to raise safety concerns than they would in a culture that discourages unsolicited information. Again, where the culture favors initiative, employees will be more likely to offer unconventional solutions than employees in a culture that favors sticking to established procedures.

Culture supports safety execution. In chapter 6 we talked about the importance of strong safety-enabling systems. These are critical but by themselves are not enough to ensure high performance. Recently, we worked with a utility organization newly formed by a merger of three separate companies. We found that the company with the strongest safety performance—over a period of years—was actually the one with the weakest safety-enabling systems. The company compensated for what would normally be a significant liability by supporting a very strong culture. Employees had a strong value for safety that dictated "doing the right thing" whether there was an explicit rule or not.

Culture is shaped by leadership. Culture changes slowly, but it is changing all the time. Leaders are always changing the culture each time they make a decision, leave an issue hanging, take a stand, or address an issue. The challenge is to direct and accelerate the natural change that is already happening.

When culture conflicts with strategy, culture wins. Culture is such a strong driver of performance because it shapes how people act and respond, particularly where rules or procedures are not clearly defined. In safety, studies have shown that two sites can have nearly identical directives, systems, procedures, and site populations, yet yield very different safety outcomes. The difference is in the culture of the unique organization.

Whether high safety performance comes easily or is almost impossible to achieve depends on the atmosphere—the organizational culture—that leadership creates. When the culture is strong, engagement and execution become easy (Table 7–1).

TABLE 7–1. The Culture Discipline.
Values, beliefs, and assumptions that influence what people do and the way they do it.

	Facet	Defined as
AVOIDANCE	Alienated	The culture values risk taking.
	Subsistent	The culture doesn't value risk taking, but it doesn't value safety either.
COMPLIANCE	Fragmented.	The organization's value for safety is cosmetic.
	Cohesive	Safety is valued for its utility to the organization.
VALUES	Implicit	Safety is valued for itself.
	Adaptive	The organization's value for safety is resilient to outside forces.

What you might see or hear

This is the quintessential "cowboy" culture. Safety is seen as a barrier to work. At the front line, people who do whatever it takes to get the job done attain hero status, even (or sometimes especially) if it involves putting themselves in harm's way. Leaders gain recognition by identifying workable shortcuts around safety requirements and costs.

In this organization, safety is a neutral concept, something tangential to the real work of the organization. Generally, people do not see the need to improve safety and express indifference to existing activities. Participating in or leading safety holds no status benefit.

Safety here is viewed largely as a hygiene factor, that is, something required of "good" organizations. People engaged in safety activities are recognized but not viewed as contributing anything of strategic value. Safety tends not to be a topic among leaders until something bad happens.

Organizations at this stage recognize the business benefits of safety and tend to frame safety activities in this context. Leaders will frequently talk about the cost of injuries, the production benefits of safe work, etc. Employees who participate in safety activities are viewed as contributing to the bottom line.

At this level of functioning, safety is seen as inherently worthwhile. The return on investment rationale for safety activities and investment is replaced by the conviction that "we just don't hurt people." Employees involved in safety activities are seen as high-value contributors. Leaders are recognized for championing safety.

At the highest levels of Culture, safety is seen as an essential business function and safety investment is treated as a non-negotiable. Employees who participate in safety are esteemed as partners in change. Leaders are recognized for developing holistic strategies that include people and safety.

Evaluating the Culture Discipline

Have you walked into a facility you have never been in before and, after being there for an hour or so, had a sense of the culture there? How do you assess it? What are the revealing things you see? Some indicators include:

- Are people talking to one another—not in idle chat but engaged in conversations about the work?

- Are first-line supervisors out on the floor instead of just hanging out in their offices?

- How do employees respond to leaders? Do people seem to duck when they see their supervisors coming?

- Is there a sense of order, e.g, is the housekeeping good?

- Do people seem to enjoy their work?

- Do you see smiles, offers of help, and people asking each other's opinion about the work?

What three words would you use to characterize the culture of your organization?

CASE IN POINT: CULTURE

Building a Shared Value for Safety

The development of the Culture discipline depends on relationships within the organization. But how do you develop the value for safety when relationships don't yet exist? This was the challenge for two global companies joined in a merger. Each brought to the new company similar safety practices and initiatives, including well-developed behavior-based safety efforts at many locations. They each also brought distinct ways of doing things.

Soon after the merger, site safety facilitators and corporate leaders partnered to form a safety networking group. The group was open to all locations in the new company, and its charter was to support the safety efforts they had in common. The group kicked off with a meeting held at a lodge selected specifically for its remote environment and minimalist amenities. As one leader put it, "You can't spend the night in your room watching television when there is no television."

The forced closeness helped the group confront some of the barriers to building a common platform for safety. In addition to talking through the uncertainty that comes with a merger, participants from some sites shared how numerous changes in ownership had made their employees hesitant to get too invested in anything, including safety. Meeting in person helped allay these concerns, especially the fear that safety efforts would suffer more dramatic change. Leaders discovered that they actually had a lot of values in common. They all shared a commitment to improving safety processes and a value for building internal expertise. Many leaders also recognized a shared bad habit of "doing everything yourself," rather than developing the expectation and value for collaboration with employees at all levels in finding safety solutions.

The group adapted a "grab, gather, give, and guts" networking practice to develop the new culture. Networking participants were expected to "grab" new expertise they identified in other groups, "gather" solutions through collaboration, "give" knowledge gleaned through their own experience, and, finally, show "guts" by relating painful lessons learned. Within a short time, the group's activities were fueling safety innovations at dozens of locations in several countries. In addition to helping people make the transition to the new organization, the group credits networking activities with raising safety issues to the corporate level as site-level facilitators now routinely partner with organizational leaders on safety performance issues.

THE LEADERSHIP DISCIPLINE

How do you lead the journey from a culture in which safety's priority changes with events (e.g., "Last week we had a serious near miss, so this week everyone is really paying attention!") to one in which the vigilance never lets up? As a leader, how do you know whether during the third shift, at three o'clock in the morning, in your most remote facility, people are making decisions by considering safety first? How do you even know where to start?

Despite the critical importance of safety leadership, many leaders don't fully recognize their own influence. This is true of organizations across much of the Zero Index spectrum but is most evident within organizations in crisis. In the aftermath of a serious event we often hear frustrated leaders say things like, "This wouldn't have happened if people would've just followed the procedures." Or, "If only our first-line supervisors would pay more attention to the guidelines." Or even, "Our safety is fine—it's those contractors who need help."

> At the end of the day, who else will make safety happen but you?

The reaction is understandable. Leaders are, after all, human—and safety issues can be highly complex. But decrying the lack of compliance, cohesiveness, or forethought does nothing to answer the fundamental question that faces any leader who truly desires change: At the end of the day, who else will make safety happen but me? From a distance, the answer seems obvious. What leaders do, say, and decide communicates to others in the organization the place safety holds in everyday priorities: What is important—and what is not. Yet the execution of safety leadership is not so simple. Many leaders, even highly accomplished executives, find that there is a wide gap between knowing that something should be done in safety and knowing what that something is.

The Leadership discipline relies first on an understanding of how leaders influence safety, which is in many ways no different from the practice of leadership elsewhere in the business. Wherever an organization "is"—with regard to fiscal health, brand recognition in the marketplace, or the value placed on the individual worker, the root cause of that current state maps back to leadership. In safety, leaders establish where the organization "is" through their influence on several key disciplines. Chiefly, leaders:

- Define the safety goal. (The Vision discipline)

- Model expectations of how people in the organization should be viewed—as commodities or as precious, intangible assets. (The Culture discipline)

- Set the course for how the organization views injury causation. If leadership isn't thinking upstream of injury, it is unlikely that anyone else will. (The Exposure discipline)

- Decide the role and funding of safety professionals as well as how their function is viewed. Are safety professionals respected players at the table? Is their advice heeded around reducing exposure? Or are they compliance police charged with ensuring that the organization stays out of trouble as much as possible? (The Expertise discipline)

- Establish what is important by the things they monitor and measure. If only lagging indicators in safety are measured, then the organization focuses its attention there—after the fact. The vision and motivation to get ahead of injuries rest with leadership. (The Scorecard discipline)

- Set the rigor of safety policies and procedures, the adherence to process safety, and the focus required every minute, every day. (The discipline of Safety-Enabling Systems)

Clearly, the Leadership discipline is about more than involving executives in safety conversations or planning. If that were the case, many more or- ganizations would perform better than they do. The Leadership discipline is much more specific: it is the rigorous and systematic application of lead- ership practices, strategy, and action to the execution of the organization's goals. The Leadership discipline is both horizontal and vertical—horizontal, in the sense that safety leadership must be developed across an organiza- tion's senior team and stakeholders in order to focus and drive safety execu- tion; and vertical, because leaders need to be developed and deployed at all levels in order to execute the organization's goals in daily working life.

The Development of Safety Leadership

Regardless of level, leadership is about seeing the right things to do to reach organizational objectives and motivating others to do these things effectively. Leadership is manifested by decision making, which is related to the beliefs of the leader and demonstrated by his or her behavior. Leadership develop- ment is in many ways highly individual to each leader, requiring attention to individual strengths and weaknesses while creating consistency and align- ment across the organization. Developing safety leadership requires:

- Educating oneself on the principles of effective safety leadership

- Developing an openness to rethinking what one is thinking

- And, most of all, challenging one's assumptions

The Principles of Effective Safety Leadership

Unlike other strategic initiatives or areas of focus, finding the platform around which to rally the troops in safety is relatively easy. No one wants to get hurt. But just as no employee gets up in the morning and says, "I think I will get hurt today," no leader gets up saying. "I think I will send mixed messages about the importance of safety." But it happens—every day—often because organizations don't understand how to lead safety or develop their principal players into effective safety leaders. We have written extensively elsewhere on the qualities, practices, and style of great safety leaders and there is a wealth of literature that describes great leadership generally.[1]

> *Developing safety leadership requires education, openness, and challenging one's assumptions.*

To summarize our earlier writings, what makes an effective safety leader? First, these best practices:

- **Vision.** The effective leader sees precisely what safety excellence looks like, articulates the vision, and conveys it in a compelling way throughout the organization.

- **Credibility.** The effective leader commands believability and trust from others in the organization, including both peers and direct reports.

- **Collaboration.** The effective leader works well with other people, promotes cooperation and collaboration in reducing exposures to hazard, actively seeks input from people on the issues that affect them, and encourages others to implement their decisions and solutions for improving safety.

- **Communication.** The effective leader is a great communicator. He or she encourages people to give honest and complete information about safety even when (or especially when) the information is unfavorable.

- **Action orientation.** The effective leader proactively addresses safety issues. He or she gives timely, considered responses to safety concerns, demonstrates a sense of personal urgency and energy to achieve safety results, and delivers results with speed and excellence.

---

1   Thomas R. Krause, *Leading with Safety*, (Hoboken: Wiley Interscience, 2005). See also:
    James M. Kouzes and Barry Z. Posner, *The Leadership Challenge* (San Francisco: Jossey-Bass, Inc., 1995);
    Bruce Avolio, *Full Leadership Development: Building the Vital Forces in Organizations*, (Thousand Oaks, CA: Sage Publications, 2004).

- **Feedback and recognition.** The effective leader provides usable feedback and recognizes people for their accomplishments.

- **Accountability.** The effective leader practices accountability. He or she gives people a fair appraisal of their efforts and results in safety, clearly communicates people's roles in the safety effort, and fosters the sense that every person is responsible for the level of safety in his or her organizational unit. This practice comes last because, absent the other practices, accountability risks becoming merely blame, which damages performance.

Second, an effective safety leader practices a transformational style which includes four dimensions:

- The Influencing dimension establishes the basic credibility and principled action critical to forming relationships.

- The Engaging dimension creates relationships that are based on mutual respect and understanding.

- The Inspiring dimension propels these relationships toward an improved future.

- The Challenging dimension helps break paradigms that get in the way.

Challenging Our Assumptions

The Leadership discipline depends on consistency and alignment among all organizational leaders. But getting there often requires rethinking how and why decisions are made as they are. One organization we worked with experienced this during an internal conference when a plant manager asked about the budget status of a planned installation of redundant lock-out/tag-out systems. One senior leader responded that the funds "probably wouldn't be cut." At an earlier time in the company's leadership development, this answer would have been the final word, and the discussion would have moved on. But this organization's leaders had made a conscious decision to rethink how they supported safety. So a more senior leader, who was heavily involved in the effort to change the organization, challenged his colleague's view.

"Actually, this is exactly what we must do—have the resolve to say that equipment without the redundant system simply won't be operated," he said. "We can't tell our employees that freeing up more dollars for other things—say, boosting the brand—is more important than their safety."

In many organizations, the term leadership is reserved for those with operational oversight of some kind. While the activities and development of leaders will vary by level, the principles of vision, action orientation, credibility, and so on, are equally important to the success of an hourly employee leading an observation process as they are to the success of the regional director. One COO we know recently shared his own epiphany in this regard after observing his organization's employee-driven safety systems. Once a quarter, this leader visits a mine and sits in on a steering committee meeting with the goal of communicating and providing his support. After a few such visits, he was astonished at the leadership talent within the hourly ranks. He saw team members who expertly articulated a vision for safety, influenced their peers in safety discussions and decisions, and challenged other leaders, including managers and the COO himself, to change their own behaviors. This COO began inviting these facilitators to present to the organization's board of directors, in effect bringing together safety leaders from everywhere in the organization.

What kinds of talent might be hidden in your organization, waiting to be unleashed?

The Leadership discipline, like all the other disciplines, can be expressed as a range (Table 7–2).

NOTES

TABLE 7–2. The Leadership Discipline.
How leadership is developed and deployed in safety.

	Facet	Defined as
AVOIDANCE	Suppressed	Attempts to improve safety are viewed as unproductive and a waste of time and money.
	Dormant	Safety is managed, not led.
COMPLIANCE	Emergent	Some safety leaders practices are used.
	Competent	There is a prevalence of safety leadership across top leaders in operational units.
VALUES	Visionary	Competent safety leadership spreads to all functional areas, to more layers of management, and there is a prominent safety vision among top leaders.
	Ubiquitous	Safety leadership is demonstrated by all employees

What you might see or hear

Safety isn't considered worth leadership attention. Lower-level leaders may be required to deal with only the most pressing safety issues as they emerge. Leadership involvement is minimal and largely reactive. Isolated attempts to advance safety performance are dismissed as unproductive. In one fast-growth company we worked with, there wasn't a safety function in the organization for the first ten years. It wasn't seen as a priority.

Basic safety management is an expectation. Leaders at all levels have minimal involvement in, or acquaintance with, safety. When leaders do engage safety performance, they direct by fiat.

Basic safety leadership is an expectation. Practices, such as accountability and feedback and recognition start to emerge among leaders at all levels, however leaders tend to be largely reactive in dealing with safety issues. Individual leaders show concern for safety, but the lack of consistent, aligned action may give the impression that safety is not a high priority. The effectiveness of the same initiatives tend to vary according to the individual leader.

Good safety leadership is formally defined within the business. Senior leaders have a clear understanding of safety functioning and where it fits within the business. Leadership development starts to emerge for safety as leaders seek out feedback and coaching on their performance.

Safety leadership is an expectation for leaders across the business. Senior leaders will seek out feedback from their colleagues and direct reports on their strengths and weaknesses relative to safety leadership and actively work toward higher performance.

Safety leadership is an expectation for employees across the business. Front-line employees will give feedback to even senior-level leaders on safety.

Evaluating the Leadership Discipline

You can assess your own organization's performance of the Leadership discipline by pondering these questions about your own organization:

- How do senior leaders talk about serious injuries and fatalities—in numbers or by names of people?

- What message do we send when we say, "We want to improve our safety performance 50% this year," if last year we had four people suffer life-altering injuries?

- When talking about production, is the conversation about safe production? In other words, do leaders, in their minds, separate the two concepts?

- Do leaders insist on including contractor safety performance in the organization's numbers with the view they are accountable for the safety of everyone on the property/site/platform?

- Would you as a leader want your son or daughter—say, on summer break from college—to work in one of your facilities in an entry-level job?

CASE IN POINT: LEADERSHIP

How Alcoa Led the Way

When Paul O'Neill joined Alcoa as CEO in 1987, he set out to let employees know that the organization cared about them. So, O'Neill did something extraordinary: he made safety outcomes the primary indicator of senior leadership's performance. O'Neill communicated that there would be no excuses when it came to safety. Safety would have no budget. He told his accountants never to show him the money saved through safety initiatives. In fact, he'd fire them for equating safety with finances, not people.

Early on, O'Neill told managers that if something needed to be fixed, he wanted it fixed immediately—no more waiting for budget approvals and hoping that nothing bad happened in the meantime. O'Neill also gave labor leaders his home phone number and told them to call day or night if managers were not living up to these expectations. Three weeks later, O'Neill received a late night call from a worker at a plant in Tennessee. A conveyer belt had been broken for three days and workers were being forced to manually hoist 600-lb ingots from one spot to another. O'Neill immediately called the plant manager. By 5am, that conveyer belt was back on line. "They soon knew I meant it," says O'Neill.

O'Neill set himself apart in other ways. When a new office was built, he eschewed the corner office for a cubicle like everyone else. In the early 1990s, he championed a little known technology called the internet, and soon employees at every site had access to information about injuries and near misses anywhere in the organization within 24 hours. He told people that safety is not a priority. "It's a precondition."

Within five years, the rate of both lost workdays and serious injuries had dropped by 50%. The emphasis on safety had also transformed the organization in other ways; employees at all levels began offering ideas for new products and new efficiencies. People listened to each other. As one leader later said, "Paul came in and got us to do things we never thought we could do."

SOURCES: Michael Arndt, "How O'Neill Got Alcoa Shining," Business Week, February 5, 2001; Mark Roth, "Habitual excellence—The Workplace According to Paul O'Neill," Pittsburgh Post-Gazette, May 13, 2012; William Bratton and Zachary Tumin, Collaborate or Perish: Reaching Across Boundaries in a Networked World, (New York: Crown Business, 2012), 203-217.

THE SUSTAINING SYSTEMS DISCIPLINE

Business systems might seem an odd place to focus safety execution. After all, what does a leader's promotion, an employee recognition program, or staffing and budget decisions have to do with safety functioning? These and other routine business processes are general to organizational functioning. But if you look more closely at how safety outcomes occur, very often the root cause of an incident may trace back years to a decision made at a very high level. Organizational systems actually have everything to do with safety—precisely because they drive the business.

Determinations about staffing levels, supervisory development, promotions, budgets, or new projects all signal what's valued and what's important. Whether intended or not, a promotion is an implicit endorsement of a person's past leadership and actions with respect to safety. Decisions about staffing or organizational structure sometimes subtly—sometimes profoundly—alter the interface between people and technology. The configuration and use of these and other business systems tell employees what is rewarded and what they are able to do.

The Sustaining Systems discipline is about the development and alignment of business processes with safety as a value and with safety targets. Fundamentally, organizational Sustaining Systems include all business processes that maintain and ensure the effectiveness of safety-enabling elements across time. These may include, but are not limited to:

- Hiring and training functions

- Performance management systems, including processes for defining individual performance expectations and tracking personal performance

- Development and succession planning

- Assignment of responsibilities and accountabilities

Providing Context and Consequence

Although most organizations have these systems in some form, their quality varies substantially. In part, this is due to their apparent remoteness from safety. Many organizations simply don't recognize the relationship of these systems to Safety-Enabling Systems, to exposure, and to safety outcomes themselves. In addition, senior leaders often perceive the Sustaining Systems as "just people systems" and abdicate them to the human resources department. What both are missing is that an organization's Sustaining Systems are among its most significant levers for changing the culture. Sustaining systems do this by:

- **Communicating what is valued.** How people are recognized, rewarded, and promoted establishes what is really important in the organization.

- **Setting expectations.** Performance management for individuals and groups shapes how people interact with safety initiatives and goals— or whether they engage them at all.

- **Providing consequences.** Rewards and recognition in particular shape people's behavior with respect to organizational goals and initiatives.

- **Supporting safety activities.** Auditing and resourcing safety systems ensures that they are enabled to function optimally.

- **Enabling participation.** Leadership training, development, and succession planning provide people with the means to do what we are asking them to do.

We have seen that organizations can run the range of the Sustaining Systems spectrum. When functioning optimally, we see systems that ensure integration of safety with the business and that support safety functioning with precision. Most organizations are somewhere in the middle, where organizational systems support safety for the most part, but varying levels of misalignment will create drag on functioning. At the extreme, organizational systems can be overtly hostile to, or in conflict with, safety goals, oftentimes because the organization has failed to recognize the profound impact these systems have on safety. The range or continuum of the Sustaining Systems discipline is shown in Figure 7–3.

FIGURE 7–3. The Sustaining Systems discipline. The organizational antecedents and consequences that support effective safety management, leadership, and performance.

	Facet	Defined as
AVOIDANCE	Heroic	Systems reward people who meet production targets and taking risks is expected.
	Punitive	Organizational systems punish employees who are injured.
COMPLIANCE	Incentivized	Organizational systems reward people or departments who do not report injuries.
	Managed	Organizational systems reward people or departments who are injury-free.
VALUES	Developed	Organizational systems reward people and departments who reduce exposure to risk.
	Aligned	In addition to being developed, the organization ensures that its structure, processes, and systems work together to support safety.

What you might see or hear

Organizational systems here are weighted to support production or profitability at any cost. Safety communication and expectations are so negligible as to be non existent. People are rewarded, evaluated, and managed based only on their contribution to the bottom line. Here you will often see leaders with poor safety records promoted because they "get the product out" and employees lauded for getting the job done, despite putting themselves or others at risk.

Organizational systems here react to accidents when they happen, but otherwise do not support safety activities. Safety communication and expectations tend to be sporadic and weak. Safety is a criterion in individual and team performance only in the context of an event. Here you will often see leaders and others faulted after an accident, yet will not be provided the support or resources to proactively lead safety.

Safety begins to emerge as a distinct, though poorly defined, performance goal. Safety communication reflects a strong focus on outcomes, particularly injury numbers, and tends to be reactive. Rudimentary roles and responsibilities hold individuals and departments accountable for injuries and rely on extrinsic motivators for compliance. Conflicting messages, such as making it required to report all incidents, however small, while at the same time offering prizes to workgroups with no reported injuries are often seen.

Safety becomes a formal part of organizational systems and an explicit expectation for individuals and workgroups. Safety communication and expectations are consistent and clear, though may at times be more aspiration than reality. Audits of safety systems and practices become more regular and begin to focus on functioning in addition to outcomes. Rewards transition away from reported injuries to the performance of safe work. You will see employees or leaders routinely recognized for leading teams or initiatives.

Organizational systems provide comprehensive support of safety functioning. Safety systems and programs are regularly reviewed for performance and reliability. Safety is a standard criterion in individual and team performance management, and people are rewarded for their contribution to reducing exposure. For example, here you will see a leader's safety record given equal weight to business performance in hiring and promotion decisions.

Organizational systems here are fluent and adaptable to changing business and exposure conditions. Both safety and business systems are routinely reviewed to assess their compatibility with each other and with the organization's safety goals. The organization includes safety in its development and succession planning.

Evaluating the Sustaining Systems Discipline

Here are some questions to consider when assessing how effectively your organization is leveraging its Sustaining Systems:

- What are the criteria for promoting an operational manager? How does his or her previous track record in safety enter into the consideration?

- How is safety consideration communicated when promotions are announced?

- How much time is spent on the on-boarding process for every new employee? What is the quality of the process? How rigorous is the safety component?

- How is leadership compensation tied to safety performance?

- Do employees receive a discretionary bonus tied to safety? What is tracked and measured? Is the bonus based on lagging or leading indicators?

- How is safety considered in contractor selection?

- How clear are people on the expectations around safety?

CASE IN POINT: SUSTAINING SYSTEMS

Rethinking Performance Management

Knowing how to drive individual and group performance is one of the perennial challenges of management. Still, few consider the effects that performance management systems can have on safety. That lesson was brought home for one U.S.-based organization we worked with when a culture assessment uncovered a low rate of injury reporting—a key indicator of safety performance.

Digging deeper, senior leaders discovered that one of the prime drivers of low reporting was the performance management system. Managers and supervisors were evaluated partly on the number of injuries that occurred within their workgroups during the year. This well-intended goal, which was designed to focus leadership on safety, was instead incentivizing managers and workgroups to either under report injuries or to creatively classify those that were reported.

The CEO took the unusual step of immediately removing injuries as a measure of manager performance across the organization. A cross-functional team developed new performance measures focused on upstream indicators that were more realistically within the control of individual managers, for example safety-supporting behaviors, team participation in safety activities, and demonstrated reductions in exposures. Not long after, the number of injuries did begin to tick up—a sign that the organization was getting a truer picture of exposures and was establishing a healthier climate for raising and dealing with safety issues.

ADVANCING THE ORGANIZATIONAL DISCIPLINES

The three Organizational disciplines—Leadership, Culture, and Sustaining Systems—are critical to driving and sustaining safety functioning. To improve performance in these disciplines, leaders need to:

- Assess the alignment of leadership around safety's role in the organization. Is there consensus about the strategic value of safety performance?

- Assess the quality, and variability, of safety leadership in the organization. Is there an explicit value for developing safety leadership? Or is it something left to develop organically?

- Discuss the net effect of the Organizational disciplines together: What values and initiatives do they collectively support?

- Assess the organization's current level of functioning in each of the disciplines.

- Evaluate how each discipline currently affects the functioning the others; for example, how does safety leadership (the Leadership discipline) influence organizational consequences provided by business systems (the Sustaining Systems discipline)?

- Assess the relationship between these disciplines and the Foundational disciplines (chapter 5) and the Safety disciplines (chapter 6). Ask: How might our current functioning in Leadership, Culture, and Sustaining Systems be shaping how we execute the other disciplines?

- Identify the beliefs and practices that are keeping performance where it is. What would we need to change to move forward?

The Organizational disciplines, more than any others, define who the organization is and how it functions. When these disciplines are weak or underperforming, it makes raising the level of all the other disciplines a very tough road.

In the last three chapters we have explored the 10 practices, or disciplines, that make up the Zero Index model, laying out the scale of performance for each. How can an organization tell how well it is performing each discipline? How can you assess where you are—and where you want to be? In the next section we begin to put the pieces together in a way that is actionable.

NOTES

PART III:

Creating the Zero Index Organization

ASSESSING WHERE YOU ARE

by Guy Boyd and Ricky Yu

ASSESSING WHERE YOU ARE

Not long ago, we received a call from the manufacturing director of a major European corporation. Bob recounted a familiar tale of attempts to reduce the unacceptable level of accidents across his EU sites. Well known for his track record in improving quality and profitability, and also for his desire to improve safety in a high-exposure industry, Bob had been headhunted for his current position two years earlier. He was a passionate advocate of injury-free culture who genuinely believed that all injuries were preventable. In the past he had implemented simple behavior-based safety programs with some success and he understood the role of leadership at all levels in improving safety performance.

So when he was recruited to the new organization, Bob brought along his former health, safety, and environment (HSE) manager. The two men quickly set about replicating the winning formula from their previous organization, which was to follow a behavior-based safety (BBS) approach: providing training courses for managers, developing core safety management systems elements, and implementing cardinal rules. However, the results didn't follow as expected. Minor safety events and more serious injuries continued to occur at a worrisomely high rate.

"Where am I going wrong?" Bob asked. "It worked well in my previous company, and this is a very similar organization—so why is it so different here?"

"Where am I going wrong?" Bob asked.

DEVELOPING YOUR ZERO INDEX PROFILE

Making safety a strategic objective usually entails considerable change in an organization, both structurally and culturally. For most organizations, reaching this desired state requires alterations that might not be immediately evident. Organizations can appear deceptively alike in their espoused values and even in their practices and rules. Understanding what makes them different—specifically, why they achieve different outcomes—has less to do with the "what" of their safety functioning than the "how."

There's no single cure for fixing all safety problems in all organizations. Just as a physician would never prescribe the same medicine for all her patients, the transformation of an organization from Avoidance-driven to Values-driven requires a custom approach, based on the exact situation at that company site. The use, reach, and effectiveness of safety processes can vary widely across sites, even within the same company. There can also be drastic differences in the quality of the culture and openness to change, in the employees' investment in safety activities, and in the scope of decision

Traditional safety assessments tend to be narrow in scope and shallow in depth.

making and action. In other words, to alter the results, we must first understand the execution of safety's many parts. We must have a full picture of the patient's present condition. Only then can we define how far away the patient is from topnotch physical condition in each aspect of his health. To find that out, we need to do a thorough assessment.

The difficulty for many organizational leaders is that traditional safety assessments tend to be narrow in scope (by auditing only safety systems or culture) or shallow in depth (by relying on blanket assumptions about a wide range of factors). As a result, safety assessments too frequently end up being a frustrating, check-the-box exercise performed only to satisfy organizational demands for quick answers.

An assessment whose purpose is to guide strategic change needs to be different from a traditional safety assessment, similar in depth and scope to the analysis we would perform when planning a high-profile engineering project. We need to collect data on the actual performance of the essential components. We need information for doing careful project planning (and scoping), securing employee buy-in, and defining how we want to get to the final destination—and the speed with which we want to travel.

The Zero Index model guides companies through their safety journey by identifying where they are in the various stages of safety functioning and then defining the path forward. It relies on experience and judgment to evaluate the as-is state of the organization, compares that with employee and manager perceptions about safety, and combines the two to define a set of anchor points. An assessment method that relied only on employee and manager perceptions would necessarily be weak, because most employees and managers have limited data on how they truly compare with world-class performers. On the other hand, an assessment method that relied only on the judgment of assessors without considering employee and manager perceptions would inaccurately measure organizational functioning dimensions, since these cannot usually be observed or discerned from written documents. The Zero Index assessment uses a combination of both.

When it comes to safety, do the perceptions of your employees and managers match?

ASSESSMENT METHODOLOGY

The goal of a Zero Index assessment is not to look for gaps in the types of systems you have in place. Instead, the objective is to compare what you say you want done versus what is actually being done right now, which gives a sense of the quality of the efforts, the reality on the ground, and the implications. The assessment requires sufficient time to engage employees at all levels and to collect the data necessary for developing a comprehensive profile. No one data point is sufficient to provide an accurate assessment of where an organization actually stands. Instead, the combination of data sources provides a well-rounded picture that supports the development of a path forward.

Although the activities involved in a Zero Index assessment (e.g., interviews, surveys, document review, site inspection) may seem similar to those of a routine audit, they can be adapted very effectively to focus on identifying the state of safety execution.

Interviews

A typical safety audit focuses on the managers, but in our opinion you should spend an equal (if not more) amount of time with the employees on the ground—supervisors, technicians, and shop floor employees. These are the folks who know how things actually work—why certain procedures are not executed well, what issues they face, etc. Obviously, due to their sheer number and other cultural considerations (such as language differences), the discussions may have to occur in small focus groups. Important considerations here are sampling (e.g., making sure all types of employees are heard from) level segregation (e.g., talking to supervisors and shop-floor employees separately), and language facilitation.

Surveys

Surveys can be a helpful way of eliciting quantifiable perceptions about safety from a large portion of the organization. In particular, there are survey tools available that measure safety-predictive factors in culture and leadership. Important considerations for survey administration include assuring an accurate sample of the organizational population (including representative responses by level, location, function, shift, etc.), technology (are the surveys administered using Web-based or paper-based questionnaires?), and accommodating different language needs.

Document Review

Echoing what was mentioned earlier, a document review that's part of a Zero Index assessment is not about simply checking whether or not certain documents are available. Rather, the focus is on uncovering the pattern that documents reveal, answering important questions, such as:

- Are action plans followed up and resolved in a timely manner?

- How are the lessons learned from the accident reports communicated throughout the organization?

- Do accident investigation reports address the interactions among the various elements (employees, technology, and process) of the working interface?[1]

Site Inspection

Site tours typically occupy a small portion of time during a Zero Index assessment, however they bring invaluable detail to the data collected from other sources. We have often seen issues that emerged in surveys and focus groups come to life in every-day situations observed during a site visit. Capturing such anecdotal data helps illustrate key themes and gives leaders a sense of how safety really works "on the ground." When time is limited, we suggest that efforts be spent on observing field practices—e.g., how does a supervisor run his toolbox meeting? Were the staff given any feedback about safe or at-risk behaviors?

ANCHORING THE ZERO INDEX DISCIPLINES

Once an organization has gathered data, each discipline can then be rated on a continuum (Figure 8-1). The higher the score, the better. Six anchor points identify the stages of development:

- Safety is a burden (0-9)—lowest

- Safety is a necessity (10-19)

- Safety is a priority (20-29)

- Safety is a goal (30-39)

- Safety is a value (40-49)

- Safety is who we are (50-60)—highest

Avoidance-driven organizations score in the 0-19 range, Compliance-driven organizations in the 20–39 range, and Values-driven organizations score between 40 and 60. An overall organizational score (the Zero Index score) can be computed by averaging the scores of the individual elements.

---

1   Our term for the environment in which exposure to hazards is created, mitigated, or eliminated, and where adverse events occur or are prevented.

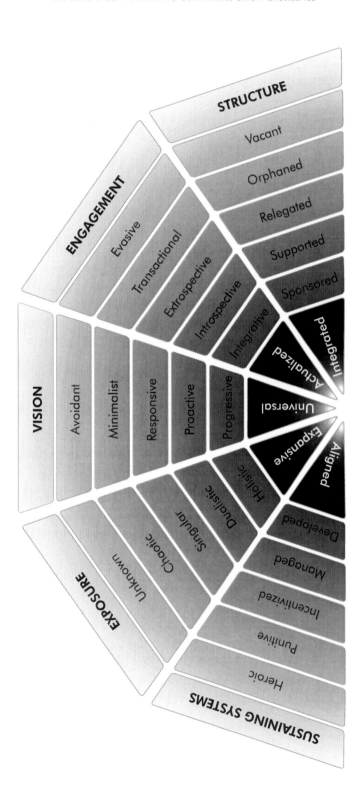

Figure 8–1. The 10 Disciplines of the Zero Index.

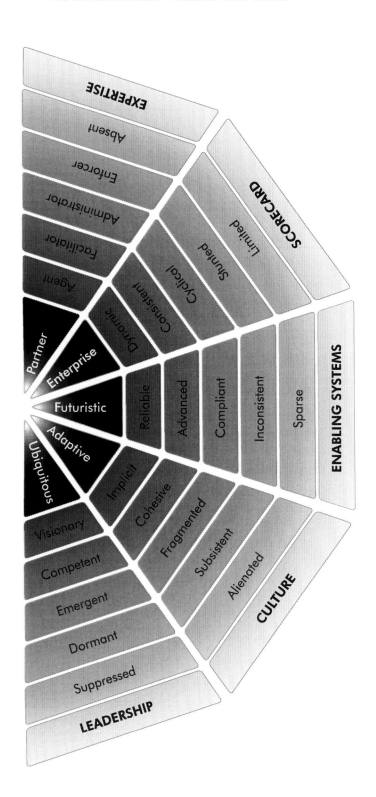

Determining your organization's level of functioning in the Zero Index model requires gathering sufficient data about the functioning of each of the disciplines. Chapters 5, 6, and 7 provided self-assessment questions to help leaders gauge roughly where they are within the Zero Index spectrum. Here we provide additional details and considerations for a more formal assessment of each discipline.

Vision

Vision is how an organization's safety vision, usually articulated by senior-most leaders, is defined and understood. An effective profile of the Vision discipline will describe how well the organization's safety goal focuses the organization's activities and strategies, reflects the organization's value for safety, and provides the motivation to improve it. Key points for assessing Vision include:

- **Goal development.** How is the documented safety goal (if there is one) established? What is it based on (i.e., a target injury rate, exposure reduction, or both)?

- **Vision development.** What is the process for establishing the safety vision?

- **Integration.** How do safety goals align with other corporate objectives?

- **Distribution.** How is the safety vision communicated? To what extent do employees at various levels know and understand the vision?

- **Weight.** What is the vision's perceived importance compared with other goals?

- **Scope.** What is the scale of the vision? What does it encompass?

Figure 8–2. Development of the Vision discipline.

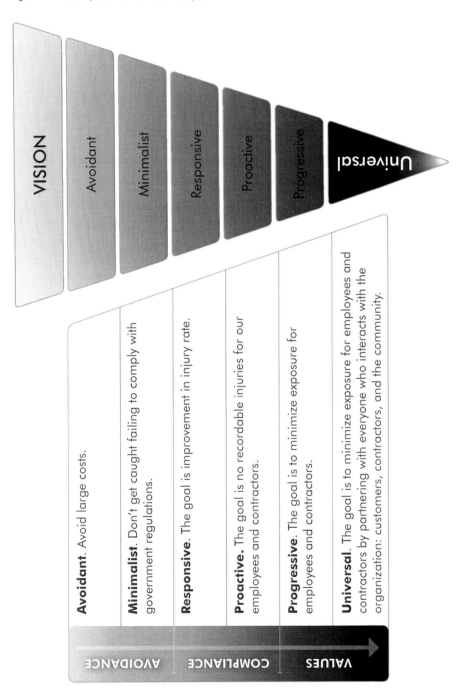

Engagement

Engagement is a measure of how people invest themselves in safety. It is a manifestation of organizational culture, reflecting the value for people and relationship within the organization. Key points to assess when developing a profile of Engagement include:

- **Organizational support.** What are employees' perceptions of the organization's concern for them—i.e., do employees believe that the company genuinely cares about them?

- **Constraint recognition.** To what extent do employees at all levels perceive that their actions make a difference?

- **Approaching others.** How do coworkers share information about safety and help each other do the job safely, both within and beyond their local work group?

- **Upward communication.** Are employees encouraged to raise safety concerns with their supervisors? Do they feel free to do so?

- **Participation.** Does the management engage employees in decision making that involves safety concerns? Do accident investigations involve employees and managers together? Do investigations look at root causes associated with management or supervisors?

- **Impact awareness.** How does the company perceive its role and its impact on the safety of external stakeholders, e.g., community, suppliers?

Figure 8–3. Development of the Engagement discipline.

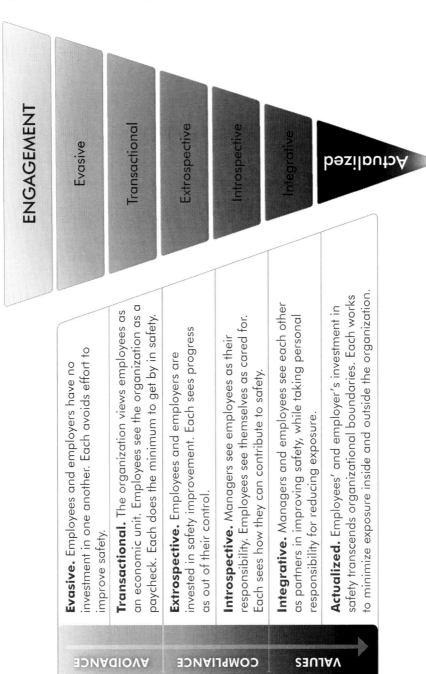

Exposure

By definition, the Exposure discipline defines how leaders think about injury causation. But this thinking plays out in how exposure reduction efforts are structured and used. The Exposure discipline can be evaluated through reviewing:

- **Investigation focus.** Do accident investigations center on conditions or worker behaviors only, or do they give sufficient attention to root causes, including leadership behavior? Also, do safety audits and inspections focus on rules and regulations or exposure and risk?

- **Follow-through.** Are actions from investigations followed up and resolved in a consistent manner? Are items highlighted during safety audits, inspections, and employee suggestion systems followed up consistently?

- **Communication.** Does management believe that all injuries are preventable? Is this communicated to all levels? Do leaders' actions align with such belief?

- **Application.** Is there a behavior-based safety process? How effective is it in addressing exposure?

Figure 8–4. Development of the Exposure discipline.

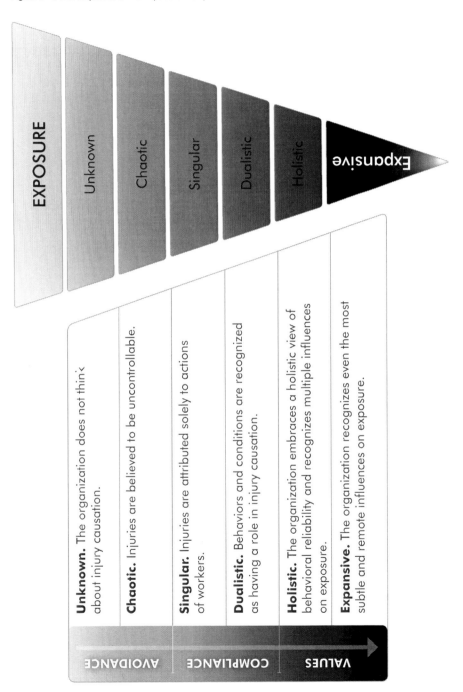

Structure

Structure is the formal framework that supports safety decision making, accountability, and action. The Structure discipline can be partly assessed through reviewing the documented roles and responsibilities that govern safety decision making. But an effective profile of this discipline digs deeper into this information by reviewing:

- **Granularity.** Who has safety goals? Safety manager? First-level supervisor? Department managers? Senior managers?

- **Goal focus.** Do safety goals focus on injury numbers/rates/costs only? Exposure reduction activities?

- **Information distribution.** Who do reports on safety performance go to? Board of directors? Senior corporate executives? Site management?

- **Safety function structure.** How are safety resources structured? To whom does the safety functional leader report? Are safety staff aligned with operational units?

- **Decision making.** Who makes what level of decisions regarding safety programs? Regarding exposure-reduction investments?

Figure 8–5. Development of the Structure discipline.

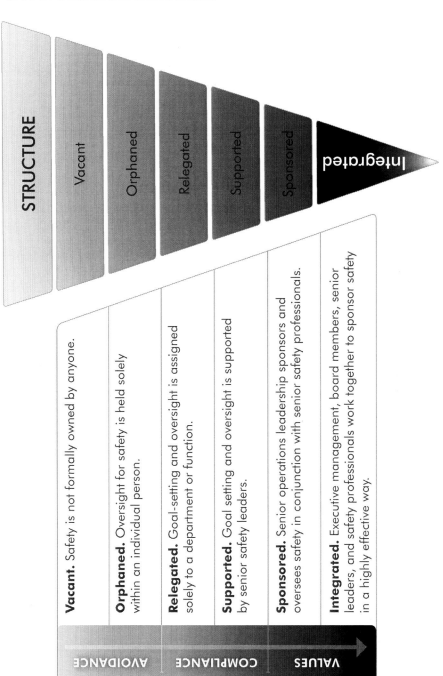

STRUCTURE

Vacant

Orphaned

Relegated

Supported

Sponsored

Integrated

Vacant. Safety is not formally owned by anyone.

Orphaned. Oversight for safety is held solely within an individual person.

Relegated. Goal-setting and oversight is assigned solely to a department or function.

Supported. Goal setting and oversight is supported by senior safety leaders.

Sponsored. Senior operations leadership sponsors and oversees safety in conjunction with senior safety professionals.

Integrated. Executive management, board members, senior leaders, and safety professionals work together to sponsor safety in a highly effective way.

AVOIDANCE

COMPLIANCE

VALUES

Expertise

The Expertise discipline reflects the position, function, and contribution of the safety professional. An effective profile of the Expertise discipline will illustrate the status of safety on the organization's agenda and serve as an indicator of how well safety is integrated with other performance areas. Organizations can evaluate the Expertise discipline by examining:

- **Role description.** Are there job descriptions for safety experts in the organization? How are the roles described?

- **Selection criteria.** What are the qualifications and selection criteria for safety experts? Do they possess the right balance of technical and business knowledge to engage other business leaders?

- **Task management.** What percentage of time do safety professionals spend on various duties (e.g., rule enforcement, training workers, creating programs, advising operations managers and supervisors, creating reports, investigating incidents, working with senior management, creating strategies)?

- **Value.** What is the perceived impact and value of safety professionals? Are safety professionals being consulted/asked for inputs in major business decisions?

- **Career path.** What is the career path for safety experts? Is there none? If there is a path, does it include advancement to larger safety responsibilities? Advancement to non-safety responsibilities? Is the career path used for the career development of high-potential executives?

Figure 8–6. Development of the Expertise discipline.

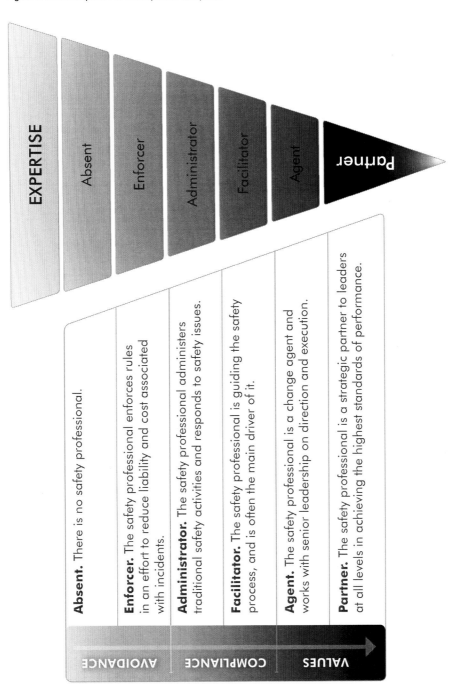

Scorecard

The Scorecard discipline reflects the way in which the organization seeks and processes information about safety. Assessing it involves a review of what measures are used, how the data are collected, and how data are used. Principally, the organization will want to review:

- **Data management.** How are data used?

- **Leading indicators.** Are leading indicators of safety performance in use? Has their validity been established? To what extent are they used to improve systems and behaviors? How inclusive are they of factors outside immediate safety systems, e.g., safety leadership?

- **Reliability.** What are the perceptions of the reliability of safety data and metrics by front-line workers? Supervisors? Managers? Senior management?

- **Injury reporting.** What is the quality of reporting of injuries and near misses? How likely are employees to report events? What are the consequences related to reporting?

Figure 8–7. Development of the Scorecard discipline.

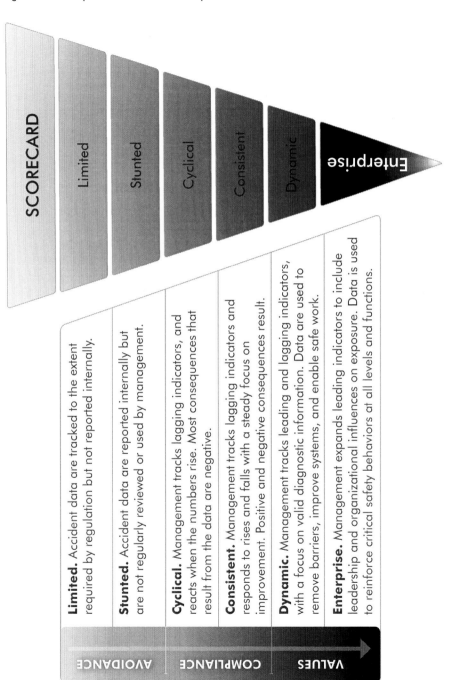

SCORECARD

Limited

Stunted

Cyclical

Consistent

Dynamic

Enterprise

Limited. Accident data are tracked to the extent required by regulation but not reported internally.

Stunted. Accident data are reported internally but are not regularly reviewed or used by management.

Cyclical. Management tracks lagging indicators, and reacts when the numbers rise. Most consequences that result from the data are negative.

Consistent. Management tracks lagging indicators and responds to rises and falls with a steady focus on improvement. Positive and negative consequences result.

Dynamic. Management tracks leading and lagging indicators, with a focus on valid diagnostic information. Data are used to remove barriers, improve systems, and enable safe work.

Enterprise. Management expands leading indicators to include leadership and organizational influences on exposure. Data is used to reinforce critical safety behaviors at all levels and functions.

AVOIDANCE

COMPLIANCE

VALUES

Safety-Enabling Systems

Safety-Enabling Systems are the specific mechanisms used to manage and improve safety. Safety-Enabling Systems cover policies and procedures, skills, knowledge, and training; hazard recognition and mitigation; and exposure reduction mechanisms. Evaluating the Safety-Enabling Systems discipline fundamentally looks at skills, competence, knowledge, process, and procedures required to work safely. A profile of this discipline should include:

- **Active systems.** What systems are provided for ensuring a safe workplace? Are key issues and exposures addressed? Do workers and supervisors perceive these systems to be used regularly?

- **Systems basis.** What is the basis of the Safety-Enabling Systems? Regulatory requirements alone? As a response to prior incidents at the location? For risk assessments?

- **High-potential exposures.** Are there life-saving rules (sometimes called cardinal rules) for exposures that have a high potential of causing life-altering injuries? Are they enforced consistently? Are SOPs periodically reviewed and updated? What can workers do if there is an imminent danger or safety concern?

- **Contractor safety.** Are there systems addressing contractor safety, and are they actively used? Is safety a criterion in contractor selection? What is the safety oversight?

- **Training programs.** What training and briefings are done routinely for existing employees? Do employees perceive these training programs and briefings to be useful and relevant?

- **Hazard recognition.** What systems and programs are in place to look for hazards and exposures in the workplace? How are the results used?

- **Reporting systems.** Is there a process for reporting safety hazards, near misses, and mishaps? Is it trusted and used? Do people who report safety issues receive feedback?

Figure 8–8. Development of the discipline of Safety-Enabling Systems.

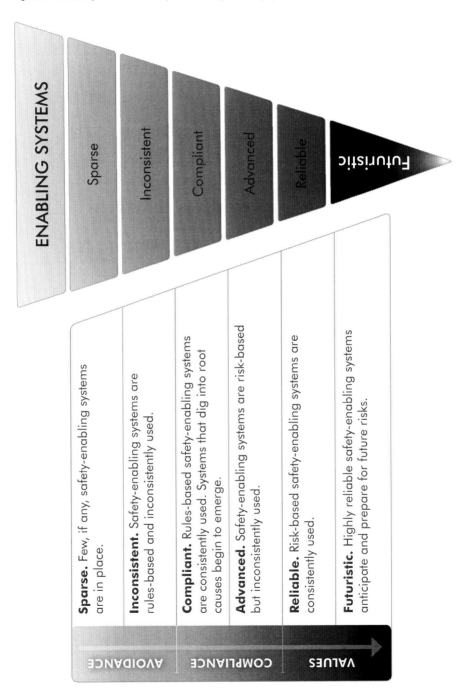

ENABLING SYSTEMS

Sparse

Inconsistent

Compliant

Advanced

Reliable

Futuristic

Sparse. Few, if any, safety-enabling systems are in place.

Inconsistent. Safety-enabling systems are rules-based and inconsistently used.

Compliant. Rules-based safety-enabling systems are consistently used. Systems that dig into root causes begin to emerge.

Advanced. Safety-enabling systems are risk-based but inconsistently used.

Reliable. Risk-based safety-enabling systems are consistently used.

Futuristic. Highly reliable safety-enabling systems anticipate and prepare for future risks.

AVOIDANCE   COMPLIANCE   VALUES

Culture

The Culture discipline reflects the values, beliefs, and unstated assumptions that influence what people in the organization do and the way in which they do it. There is a rich body of research on the organizational characteristics that support high performance in safety and other critical business functions.[2] Diagnostic work on these dimensions can supplement the development of a Culture discipline profile that examines:

- **Safety's value.** How important is safety to the organization as perceived by various levels: Senior management? Middle management? First-level supervisors? Front-line workers?

- **Safety's role.** What is the tradeoff between production and safety as perceived by various levels?

- **Deviation threshold.** How often do employees take short-cuts from established safety and operating procedures as perceived by various levels?

- **Variability.** Has the organization's attention to (or investment in) safety varied during ups and downs of business cycles as perceived by various levels?

- **Investment.** How have safety expenditures changed year-to-year for the last three years?

- **Integration.** Is safety an integral part of key business discussions, such as capital expenditure review and succession planning?

---

2   See, for example:
       Gerald R. Ferris, "Role of Leadership in the Employee Withdrawal Process: A Constructive Replication," *Journal of Applied Psychology*, 70 (1985): pp. 1075-1089.
       Jacqueline A-M Coyle-Shapiro and Neil Conway, "Exchange Relationships: An Examination of Psychological Contracts and Perceived Organizational Support," *Journal of Applied Psychology*, 90 (2005): pp. 774-781.
       Mary A. Konovsky and S. Douglas Pugh, "Citizenship Behavior and Social Exchange," *Academy of Management Journal*, 27 (June 1994): pp. 656-669.

Figure 8–9. Development of the Culture discipline.

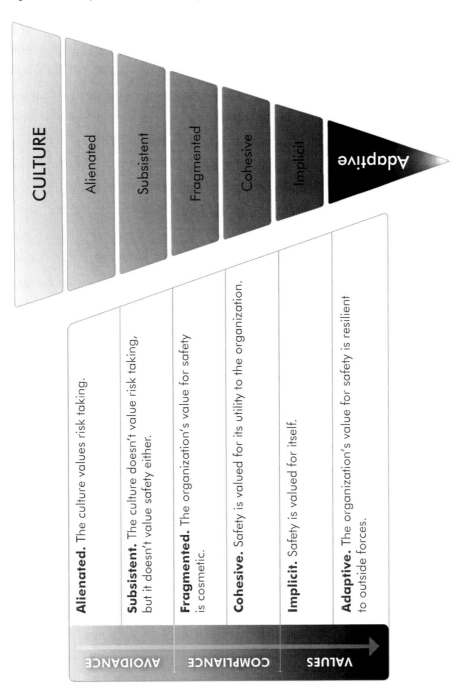

Leadership

The Leadership discipline reflects how all leaders in the organization are developed and deployed in safety. The profile of the Leadership discipline focuses on:

- **Leadership vision.** To what extent are leaders able to describe their safety vision and how it aligns with the organization's goal? How well is vision expressed at each level of leadership, e.g. among senior managers/senior executives, middle managers, and first-level supervisors respectively?

- **Strategy.** Is there an actual safety strategy or only an accumulation of programs?

- **Safety communication.** How do leaders actively communicate about safety—e.g., in stand-alone communications? By integrating safety messages into other communications?

- **Expectations.** Has the organization defined what good leadership looks like? Have leadership skills been measured either for individuals or across the organization as a whole?

- **Best practices.** To what extent do leaders use the practices related to safety performance? For example, do they walk the talk in safety-related matters?

- **Action orientation.** Are leaders proactive rather than reactive when responding to safety concerns? Do they demonstrate a sense of personal ownership, urgency, and passion? Do people at different levels take the initiative when it comes to solving, highlighting, and reporting safety issues?

- **Informed.** How informed is management about safety issues—in particular, about significant exposures? Are they aware of the most recent serious incidents?

Figure 8–10. Development of the Leadership discipline.

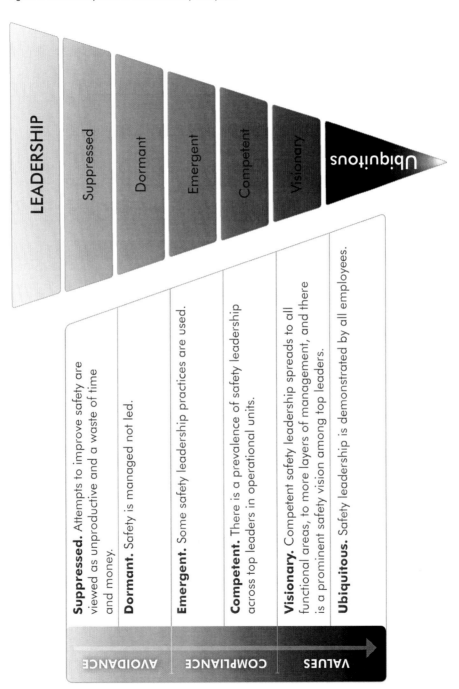

Sustaining Systems

The discipline of Sustaining Systems refers to the organizational antecedents and consequences that support effective safety management, leadership, and performance. Sustaining systems include the selection and development of people, organizational structure, performance management, and rewards and recognition. Assessing the Sustaining Systems discipline focuses on gathering data about:

- **People management.** How do safety concerns factor into the selection of contractors and the hiring and promotion of workers?

- **Safety communication.** How does safety-related communication occur across levels and functions?

- **Roles and responsibilities.** Is the responsibility for safety clearly assigned at various organizational levels?

- **Rewards and recognition.** What forms of safety recognition or awards are used in the organization? What are the criteria? How are the awards perceived? Are they valued and appreciated or seen as meaningless or mere tokenism? Do incentive programs exist at the hourly level? If so, on what are they based?

- **Performance management.** Does the performance evaluation system at each level include consideration of safety? What criteria are used? How is this element of performance evaluation perceived—as meaningful or tokenism?

- **Discipline.** Is there a discipline policy? If so, when applied to safety, is the policy well understood by workers and supervisors? Is it applied consistently (i.e., with no favoritism)? Is the policy applied for all violations or only after an injury?

- **Accountability.** Are supervisors and managers held accountable for the safety performance of their teams?

Figure 8–11. Development of the Sustaining Systems discipline.

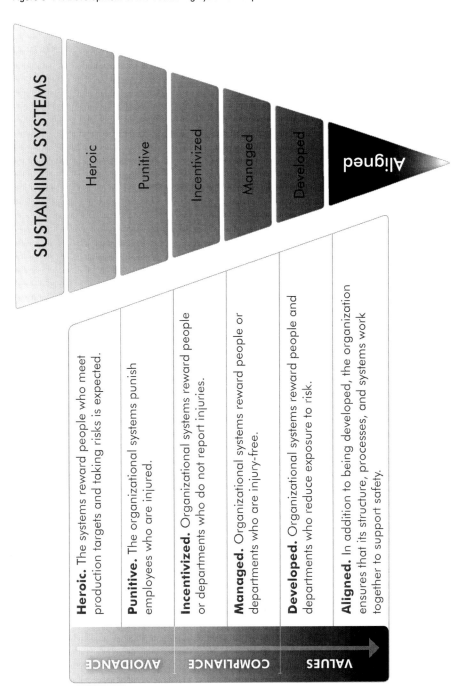

SUSTAINING SYSTEMS

Heroic

Punitive

Incentivized

Managed

Developed

Aligned

Heroic. The systems reward people who meet production targets and taking risks is expected.

Punitive. The organizational systems punish employees who are injured.

Incentivized. Organizational systems reward people or departments who do not report injuries.

Managed. Organizational systems reward people or departments who are injury-free.

Developed. Organizational systems reward people and departments who reduce exposure to risk.

Aligned. In addition to being developed, the organization ensures that its structure, processes, and systems work together to support safety.

AVOIDANCE

COMPLIANCE

VALUES

UNDERSTANDING YOUR PROFILE

The first step to improvement in any undertaking is understanding where the problem lies. Although we may often have a general sense that our culture isn't great or that our safety systems don't function effectively, what we usually don't understand is why. This can lead us to develop solutions or implement strategies that focus only on those systems—without recognizing that the problem may largely be elsewhere. We have often seen organizations strive to change a mistrustful or ambivalent culture by developing a new vision or promoting a catchy slogan while completely missing the true driver of the cultural state: conflicting signals (spoken and unspoken) emanating from its leaders.

A good Zero Index assessment reveals not just the how but also the why.

A good Zero Index assessment not only reveals the actual state of functioning (i.e., "how" the culture is not doing great) but also provides a picture of why that is the case. Understanding the results of your assessment begins by looking at three key aspects of your profile: the as-is state, where you are in the spectrum, and the degree of coherence. Figure 8-12 (right) shows a sample Zero Index assessment profile.

Your As-Is State

Your scores across the six anchor points (starting at the bottom with Safety is a burden through Safety is who we are) give you a sense of how your organization is functioning across the 10 Zero Index disciplines right now. The profile's granularity allows you to identify those characteristics that define your current state and how they are manifested in day-to-day operations.

Placement in the Spectrum

Knowing the as-is state is useful only within the context of what is possible. A full Zero Index profile helps you plot your organization's development relative to the next highest state of functioning (and the next lowest) toward the ultimate goal of achieving zero harm performance.

Degree of Coherence

Perhaps most important to planning your change strategy is understanding the relationships among the 10 disciplines in your profile. Fundamentally, a Zero Index assessment provides an at-a-glance view of your current functioning. Your profile includes an overall organizational score (the Zero Index score) that broadly defines your organization, but the particular anchors of each discipline will vary depending on your unique organization. Very rarely will an organization show perfect alignment around their overall score. For

Figure 8–12. Sample Zero Index Assessment Profile.

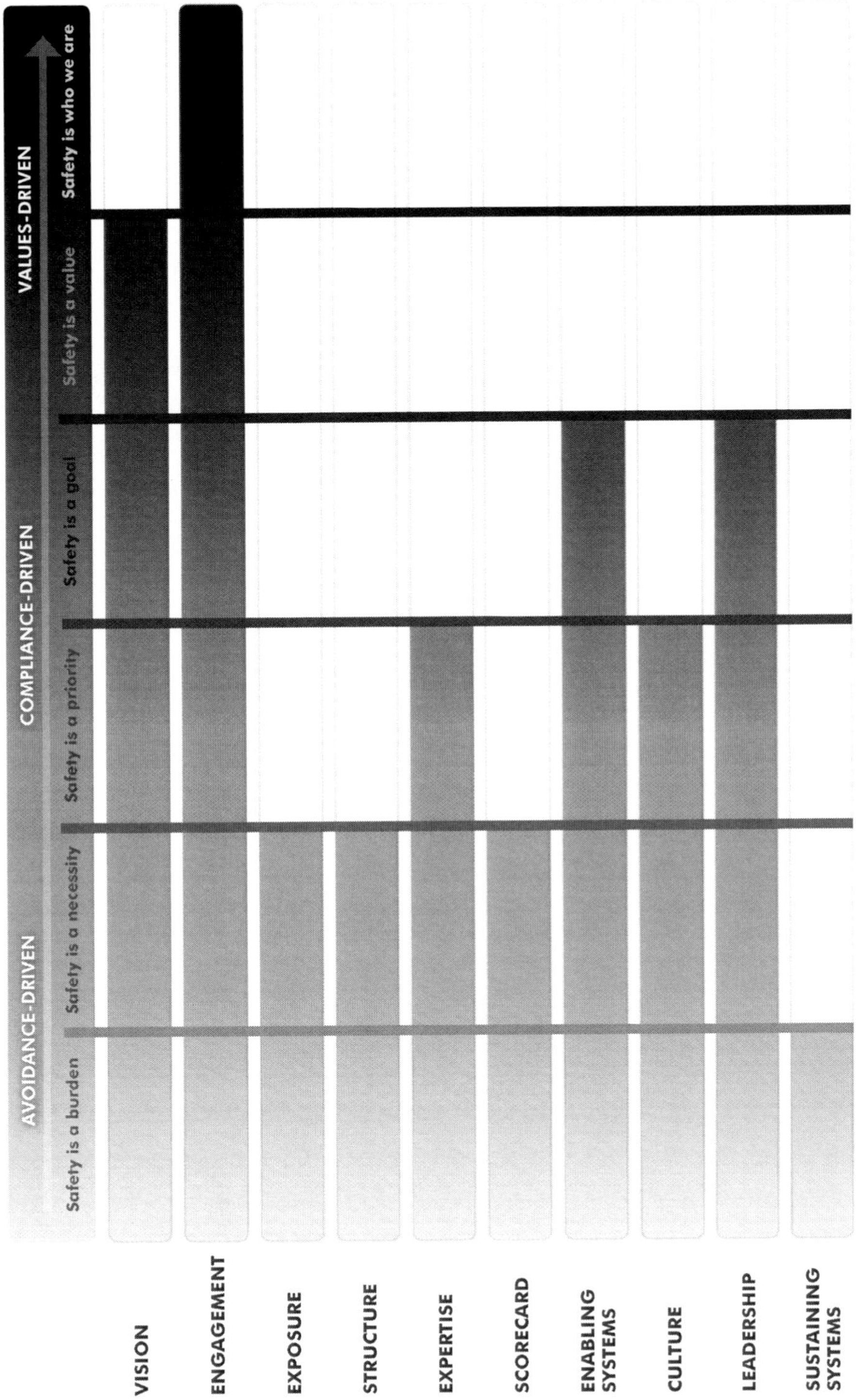

instance, an organization with a Zero Index score of 25 (Safety is a priority/ Compliance-driven) can have individual disciplines ranked in the Avoidance-driven and Values-driven ranges.

In many organizations, the disciplines will range across the anchor immediately to the left and right of the centerline. In some organizations, the anchor spread may span the whole Zero Index spectrum. The nature of the spread in itself can point to the next step. If your profile shows high dissonance (a wide anchor spread), this suggests that the first target of your change strategy is achieving coherence with the highest anchor points on your profile—in other words, bring up your lowest scores first. The strategy is similar to how a student would go about achieving a 4.0 grade point average. Instead of trying to improve in the two classes where he has a 3.5, a prudent advisor would suggest that the student start by raising the average of the classes in which he has a 2.0.

Bring up your lowest scores first.

PREPARING FOR CHANGE

So what became of Bob, the manufacturing director whose success at his prior organization couldn't be easily replicated in his new one? We spent time, over several weeks, with Bob and his team, listening and discussing the issues. The Zero Index model was critical in helping him understanding exactly why, as he put it, "It was so different here." The model helped him think in new ways and discover new insights.

As it turned out, for years Bob's organization had been heavily focused on production and profit; safety had never become a priority, let alone a core value. The resulting culture simply did not allow Bob's laudable efforts to gain any real traction, despite his passionate personal leadership. Site managers had started to understand their role in safety, but couldn't pinpoint for their direct reports the specific behaviors that would signal real change. Supervisors and middle managers were still wholly engrossed in the old production mentality. Historically, when new safety management systems had been introduced, including the simple BBS initiative, it was done with knowing winks all round: "Legally, we've got to tick the boxes, but we all know production's the only game in town…"

Most unexpected—and painful for Bob's HSE manager—was the discovery that, deep in the culture of the organization, the HSE function lacked any credibility or clout. Previous HSE leaders had been compliance-driven box-tickers, and HSE had become the place where failed leaders were "dumped" before their final demise.

Bob understands that there is still much to be done, but at least he now has a sound baseline from which to work. He has also created a truly holistic roadmap for safety that he is now—typically—driving in his accustomed relentless fashion. Bob knows that safety is a journey. Critical though they may be, gaining a solid understanding of where you are at the outset (from the broadest possible perspective) and then developing a comprehensive roadmap are just the beginning.

The Zero Index model encompasses cultural and organizational elements that influence performance across the business, not just those systems traditionally associated with safety management. The results can be eye-opening —and sometimes unsettling. Many leaders are not used to seeing safety framed in such broad terms. Bringing an open mind to the Zero Index assessment's results and recommended changes is essential. Treat the assessment as a mirror reflecting back your performance as leaders shaping the culture. A positive attitude, rather than wasting energy in defending why the scores were low, will be a giant step forward in improving management credibility. World-class management teams own the action-planning process as much as the actions themselves.

How prevalent is box-ticking in your organization?

There is always the temptation to rush to the destination (Value-driven performance) as fast as possible, but we (and Bob) would argue that identifying the most suitable path forward is more important. Keep in mind that the route to Zero Index is not static: you need to be ready to review, revise, and adjust your course.

NOTES

FROM
CONCEPT
TO REALITY

by James F. Huggett and Theodore D. Apking, Ph.D.

FROM CONCEPT TO REALITY

Getting performance from "Safety is a burden" to "Safety is a priority" all the way up to "Safety is who we are" is, at its core, a change management process. Oftentimes this process requires a redefinition of how the organization executes safety—no easy task. The realities of organizational life mean that, at any one time, the typical leader has dozens of demands on his or her time and attention. Employees must satisfy various priorities with limited resources, and everchanging business realities mean that the organization is continually adapting.

Not surprisingly, achieving excellence in execution is highly valued, whether the goal is safety performance improvement or another corporate priority. In a 2010 Conference Board survey, over 400 global CEOs, presidents, and chairmen ranked "excellence in execution" and "consistent execution of strategy by top management" as their top two concerns—more important than sustained top-line growth, customer loyalty/retention, profit growth, and improved productivity.[1] Fundamentally, execution comes down to the "how" question: How does a leadership team operationalize a true value for safety? How must leaders behave in order first to enable and then sustain the transformation?

Execution comes down to how leaders must behave in order to enable and sustain transformation.

Many organizations have historically approached safety as a tactical activity. Senior leaders ensure that competent safety professionals are in place and the leaders provide financial and other resources as necessary. Then, leaders review incident data in the monthly senior team meetings. If the safety performance data indicate no exceptional activity, they move on to the next item on the agenda. If the data skew beyond an expected range—or, heaven forbid, a serious incident or accident occurs—the leaders deploy someone to analyze root causes and "fix it," and then things gradually return to normal.

But as you read the previous chapters, it no doubt occurred to you that transforming an organization to one in which "Safety is who we are" cannot be accomplished through traditional tactical activities. For instance, aligning your Safety-Enabling Systems and Sustaining Systems with your value for safety may come about through a tactical approach. However, identifying and aligning the relevant elements within your culture—and then sustaining

---

1   The Conference Board, CEO Challenge 2010, February 2010, p.5. Viewed at www.conference-board.org.

them until they become "Safety is who we are"—is likely to require a significant change in the attitudes and behaviors of everyone in the organization (for example, formally recognizing safety contributions in performance management systems). As with any significant organizational change, creating an organization in which "Safety is who we are" will come about only through a comprehensive and strategic methodology that is driven from the top and engages everyone in the organization. In other words, transformation cannot simply be managed—it must be led.

Moving an organization from a current state to a desired future state is, by definition, a change process or transformation, and all change processes follow (or should follow) a simple template:

- First, the change leaders identify and articulate the goal or desired future state.

- Then, the change leaders assess the current state of the relevant elements within the organization.

- With that in hand, the change leaders identify the gaps between where the organization is today and where they want it to be in the future.

- Then, they develop and execute plans to close the gap.

- Finally, as many have learned over the past 30 years, leaders must sustain the process by monitoring progress and continually providing feedback and coaching to those involved. Otherwise, they risk the perception of another "flavor-of-the-month" program that reduces the credibility of management and makes all subsequent change efforts harder to deploy toward a successful outcome.

The objective of the change management process described here is to help the organization create a strategy that advances the 10 disciplines of the Zero Index model.

What distinguishes a strategic approach to safety from a more tactical approach is, specifically and unavoidably, the actions of the leaders. What leaders do—what steps they take and what words they speak—will either lead to a sustained change or a wave of activity that comes and goes without lasting impact.

Through our extensive work in supporting senior leaders as they strive to create continuous safety performance improvement, we have identified, refined, and codified a series of nine work streams (Figure 9–1). These work streams enable the breakthroughs in safety performance that senior leaders seek. For the sake of clarity, we present these work streams in a sequence that has a natural and obvious logic. However, this sequence is not intended to be a step-by-step instruction guide. Depending on your current situation, some work stream activities may already be under way. Other activities might be better conducted in a different sequence. Still others, such as internal communications and measurement, may be ongoing throughout the implementation (or, indeed, forever).

Figure 9–1. The Nine Work Streams.

1	Establish the Platform
2	Define the Current State
3	Establish Governance
4	Assess the Current State
5	Plan the Execution
6	Measure and Evaluate
7	Identify Strategic Wins
8	Deploy
9	Align and Sustain the Initiative

WORK STREAM 1: ESTABLISH THE PLATFORM

The goal of work stream 1 is to create a shared understanding of what you are trying to accomplish. The first activity for the senior leadership team is self-education—gaining a shared understanding of the concepts that are fundamental to creating a Zero Index organization. The relationship between safety systems and safety performance is obvious. However, the connection between safety performance and culture—and the critical role that leaders play in forming the right culture—tends to be less intuitive. Although the safety systems provide the tools for safe behavior, it is the culture that determines whether those tools are used when no one is being observed. And the only leverage that an organization has to achieve continuous safety performance improvement is through effective leadership. Without this fundamental understanding of the relationship between safety

Culture determines whether the safety tools are used when no one is looking.

and culture, and the role of leadership in framing culture, it can be difficult for leaders to understand how their own words, behaviors, and decisions affect and influence safety performance within the organization.

WORK STREAM 2: DEFINE THE STRATEGY

It's not uncommon for leaders to initiate a change process, and especially a safety performance improvement process, based on dissatisfaction with the current performance. After all, if your people are getting hurt on the job, what you really want is for that to stop. But just telling people that they should stop getting hurt is a less than effective strategy—otherwise, your workplace would already be injury-free. A more relevant question is: What will it look like around here? What will people be doing in the desired future that is different from what they are doing now? What are the behaviors that will create the

> In your behavioral vision of your organization's desired future, what will people be doing differently?

kind of environment in which safety is "the way we do things here"? What is our vision for the desired future of safety within the organization?

Most of us have worked through traditional visioning processes, in which we are asked to develop statements that define an idealized future. As painful as they can be, there is certainly value in developing a high-level statement of where we are headed, such as "Everyone goes home the way they came to work." But in order to truly influence behavior throughout the organization, we suggest a process we call behavioral visioning. In addition to the esoteric language of traditional visioning, behavioral visioning calls for leaders and employees to identify the specific behavioral narratives that embody safety-promoting conduct, from the boardroom to the working interface. The resulting future-state document provides behaviorally-specific descriptions that allow everyone in the organization to visualize their roles in making the future state happen.

One of the most effective ways we have accomplished this is by reading the appropriate preamble, goal, or short description of the desired state to the participants, and then simply asking the question, "If, two years from today, we were to walk through your facility, and this desired state truly existed, what would we see? How would we know?" You often hear answers such as "People will stop work when they see exposure increase," or "Leaders will regularly talk about safety." A behavioral vision identifies observable, measurable, and replicable behaviors for each level of the organization. While communicating the organization's value for safety, the document lays out behavioral expectations for every member of the organization.

WORK STREAM 3: ESTABLISH GOVERNANCE

As with any significant strategic change, achieving safety excellence requires a hands-on role for senior managers. Most leaders are familiar with the role of safety spokesperson—they're comfortable in the bully pulpit, being the cheerleader for safety. They acknowledge they must allocate resources, both time and financial, to overseeing the transformation they seek. They know they are responsible for developing and communicating the vision, identifying appropriate leading and lagging metrics, evaluating the current state, and identifying gaps between where they are today and where they want to be. They know they must develop and oversee the execution of plans to close the gaps and then ensure it all stays on track and is sustained.

Realistically, however, members of the senior leadership team can't do all of this without support. To oversee this safety transformation, leaders of larger organizations do what they often do with successful strategic initiatives: they charter an ad hoc team (the safety oversight team). This team takes charge of the planning and tactical activities and presents recommendations to the senior leadership team for its approval (Figure 9–2). A member of the senior leadership is appointed as a champion to advise and support the work of the safety oversight team.

The roles and tasks of the safety oversight team are defined in a charter document and usually include:

- Gathering and analyzing current state data related to the 10 Zero Index disciplines, e.g., Safety-Enabling Systems, Sustaining Systems, and Culture.

- Conducting a gap analysis and developing implementation plans for the approval of the senior leadership team.

- Identifying appropriate outcome and process metrics.

- Overseeing the development of methods to gather and compile the data used by the senior team and throughout the organization to monitor the progress of the initiative.

- Developing an ongoing, two-way communication process to support the change.

Figure 9–2. Transitional Governance Structure.

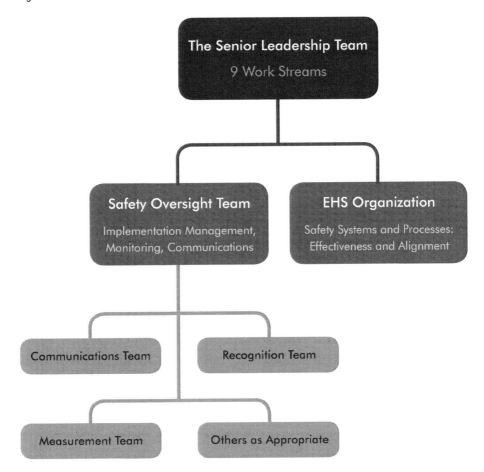

When contemplating a governance structure for the transformation, two other issues should be considered. Traditionally, the role of safety professionals—sometimes called the Environmental, Health, and Safety (EHS) organization—is to oversee the acquisition and implementation of Safety-Enabling Systems. At this juncture, the senior leadership team should discuss, clarify, and communicate what role it would like the EHS professionals to play. Although the safety oversight team is primarily focused on change management—i.e., establishing a value for safety—its duties are likely to overlap with those duties of EHS. There will certainly be confusion throughout the organization if this delineation of responsibilities is not addressed and clearly communicated early on in the process.

The second consideration is to define clearly the lifespan of the safety oversight team. At some time in the future, after the change management plans are developed and deployed, line managers must unequivocally own and take accountability for the safety performance of their organizations. We generally recommend that the charter for the safety oversight team include a sunset clause to avoid creating a shadow safety governance structure. The role of the safety oversight team is to support the transition, not to oversee ongoing safety performance improvement.

If the roles of the temporary change management team and permanent EHS organization are not clearly delineated and communicated, confusion will reign.

WORK STREAM 4: ASSESS THE CURRENT STATE

Before the organization can develop the change strategy, the senior leadership team and the safety oversight team must gain a clear and shared understanding of the current state of safety within the organization. In most cases, the task of gathering relevant data related to safety performance is included in the charter of the safety oversight team. The safety oversight team will review assessment data already in hand, note where data are insufficient, and develop plans to acquire sufficient data to truly understand the current state of safety within the organization. The assessment described in chapter 8 provides an excellent starting point.

The safety oversight team will normally oversee the gathering of the necessary data, compare the current state data with the desired future state as described in the behavioral vision, and then identify and prioritize the gaps. This analysis is then presented to the senior leadership team as a preliminary step in the planning process.

WORK STREAM 5: PLAN THE EXECUTION

When the assessment has revealed the gaps between the current state and the desired state, the organization can now craft and execute a strategy. As the entity that is most familiar with the gap analysis, the safety oversight team, or a sub team under their direction, is usually tasked with developing an initial draft of the high-level implementation plan. This draft plan is then presented to the senior leadership team for modification and approval as appropriate.

Plans at this level should set the goals and standardize the general approach without being overly detailed. At least in larger organizations, specific action plans should be developed at the site level consistent within an overall framework developed for the whole organization. But regardless of the specific plan, several fundamental components are essential.

The plan should include a clearly defined, two-way, communication process for the whole organization. Communicating the behavioral vision, and helping everyone to understand his or her role in safety fully, is only part of the objective. Another important part is creating an internal dialogue around safety that will allow leaders to adjust the plan based on real-time input from those at the working interface. In addition, the plan should identify and allocate the resources (human, time, and financial), as appropriate, to support the implementation.

WORK STREAM 6: MEASURE AND EVALUATE

Most organizations tend to have a dashboard or scorecard of performance measures that allow them to monitor safety performance across the organization. Outcome metrics, such as incidence rates or OSHA recordable rates, are typically reviewed periodically by senior leaders as part of their oversight responsibilities. While these post-event metrics are important, they tend

The more successful you are at safety, the less you can rely on traditional indicators such as injury rates.
to be insufficient. Measures that tell you what happened in the past do not always provide the information necessary to preventing the next event. Thus, leaders spend more time reacting to events and closing "barn doors" than looking for ways to prevent the next event.

When deploying a change plan, leaders must not only pay attention to safety performance but also evaluate the effectiveness of the change plan and its implementation while it is happening. The elements of the plan become the leading indicators of safety performance. For example, if the plan calls for leadership skills training for supervisors, the number of supervisors trained is an outcome measure, not just for the plan but also for the process—which becomes a leading measure for safety performance.

Creating a comprehensive set of metrics becomes even more critical as performance improves. The more successful you are at safety, the less you can rely on traditional indicators such as injury rates. A balanced dashboard of metrics that provide both outcome performance data and predictive data will allow leaders to get out in front of incidents and focus on prevention rather than incident analysis. The most sophisticated safety dashboards allow leaders to review graphic displays, which highlight statistically significant trends over time.

Best Practice: Lead from Within

Safety leadership isn't just initiatives and numbers. It's personal. As many leaders have learned, people remember most what you do in situations involving people and principles—whether (and how) you approach employees working at-risk, or challenge decisions that increase exposure, or respond to a crisis.

Developing the strength to do the right thing in these moments comes from having a clear and unshakable emotional commitment. In other words, to lead safety well, you first need to care about it. The value for safety is something we all have. It may be dormant or poorly defined, but it is something we can awaken. Start by asking yourself three questions:

- **What does safety really mean to me?** Not, what do I think safety should mean, but what does it actually mean? Is it each person looking out for each other? Making sure every person goes home the same way they came to work? Looking out for others the way I would want others to look out for my family?

- **What do I want my actions to say about my belief in safety?** Do I want people to know that I'm sincere and passionate about safety? Do I want people to know I really care? That I "have their back"?

- **What do I want people to know about their out-of-bounds behavior when it occurs?** Imagine walking into a situation where people are ignoring an exposure, either explicitly or implicitly. What do I want people to know about why I'm intervening? What values do I appeal to in the people I'm addressing—a sense of shared responsibility, the importance of looking out for each other, or something else?

Cultivating a deep emotional commitment to safety is essential to effectively leading it. Without that foundation, we won't be able to intervene when we need to—and we will struggle to create the kind of lasting change we seek. Drawing on that personal value as the source of all your safety actions, decisions, and communications is what it means to lead from within.

WORK STREAM 7: IDENTIFY STRATEGIC WINS

The process of creating an environment in which "Safety is who we are" is primarily one of changing the way people think about their roles in the organization. And, as discussed above, achieving safety excellence is a result of effective and sustained leadership behavior. However, this leads to a challenge.

Getting the leadership team to personally engage and get ready to lead the process, developing and deploying the change plan takes time—time during which people are still exposed and susceptible to injury. In response, we recommend an "early win" strategy. By identifying areas of the organization with the greatest exposure and immediately applying safety methods and tools to minimize exposure, you can reduce injuries while the change plan is still being developed and deployed.

What could be targets for your early wins?

These strategic wins are powerful because of their immediacy. They address the need to reduce injuries while you prepare your longer-range improvement plan. In addition, early results or impact create visible outcomes that leaders can use in company communications to build further support for change, helping to win over any skeptics.

One caveat, however: strategic wins typically focus on Safety-Enabling Systems, and have an immediate impact on safety performance at the targeted locations. However, they are unlikely to change permanently the way people think about their roles in safety and thus tend not to be sustainable. Unless the leadership, cultural, and other gaps are addressed, when the pressure for immediate performance improvement comes off, exposure and risk are likely to return to pre-intervention levels.

WORK STREAM 8: DEPLOY

As with any strategic initiative, the leadership team has the critical role of overseeing the development and deployment of the change plan. However, trying to change the way people think about safety, as well as what they do about safety, calls for additional considerations. Instilling new attitudes into an existing organization requires a conscious, concerted, and personal leadership effort.

The first words out of every leader's mouth will need to reinforce the message that safety is not a "priority"—it is a core value. Priorities change based on shifting business exigencies, values do not. "Safety is the way things are done here." Delivering a message on productivity? Reinforce the message that the goal is not to "be productive and be safe." By definition, being productive includes being safe. Talking about cost control? Reinforce the message that safety is not for sale. Keep in mind that everyone in the organization is evaluating the depth of your commitment based on their interpretation of your message. Be specific, be unambiguous, and integrate your safety message into every communication. Culture will not change if people believe that they can outlast it.

> **What led you to your personal value for safety?**

When you talk about safety, make it personal. Leave behind the metrics-based language of the boardroom and adopt the language of your values. Rather than referring to "incident rates" and "recordables," talk about "people getting hurt." How many people are hurt when you have an incident rate of 1.5? It is not a statistical calculation to them. Tell the personal stories that have led you to your personal value for safety. Your stories will convince people that you mean it and that your rhetoric is not just part of your annual incentive plan. If your employees believe your value for safety is personal to you, the value is more likely to become personal to them.

WORK STREAM 9: ALIGN AND SUSTAIN THE INITIATIVE

Most of us have had experience with change programs that start with great promise and then fade away over time. Speeches are made, processes are reengineered, and recognition plans are launched. But after the initial gains, the focus of the organization begins to shift to other priorities. The early progress begins to drift back to the pre-intervention levels, managers become distracted, and the perception is reinforced that employees can, once again, wait out this "flavor of the month."

Achieving safety excellence is like bending wood. Apply heat and pressure and the wood will bend. Sustain the pressure long enough and the wood will stay bent. But remove the pressure before the change is fully integrated into the fibers of the wood, and it will snap back. The challenge for leaders is to continue to keep the pressure on the safety climate, monitoring and providing feedback on the behaviors that are critical to success. By doing so, the climate they have created becomes "just the way we do things around here," leading to a healthy safety culture. In a world where challenges come at an organization in unrelenting waves, keeping the focus on any change initiative can be daunting. But when the change requires a realignment of the culture, sustaining the focus is not optional.

Simply stated, if leaders want to change the way everyone in the organization thinks about safety, the leaders will need to change the way they think about change themselves. When you read statements in change management articles such as, "It will take five years to change your safety culture," the authors are not talking about changing systems and procedures. They are referring to the time it will take for people to stop making decisions based on risk and, instead, to start instinctively doing the right thing, because "that's the way we do things around here."

Best Practice: Create a Dialogue

We often find the most significant challenge senior leaders face in safety is knowing what data should be available to them—and what questions to ask about that data. The best kind of information gathering in safety is an ongoing conversation. As leaders gain fluency in safety, their credibility rises, as does the understanding of those around them about what is important. The dialogue matures into a dynamic information flow that reflects actual conditions. This is what allows organizations to grow beyond the limitations of lagging indicators and leverage safety as strategy. There are several things leaders can ask, and create dialogue about, to begin this kind of communication:

- **Exposure to life-altering events.** While unlikely or infrequent, leaders must pay attention to events that have the potential for significant loss of life or property.

- **Upstream causal factors.** There are many things in the organization that can precede risk, from design processes to management decision making. Leaders need to be attentive to these systemic factors and know how they are influencing exposure.

- **Safety system configuration.** What are the standard disciplines required to manage safety? Leaders must understand if their organization has in place the correct management systems, disciplines, and oversight, and in the right mix.

- **Safety system performance.** Aside from the "right systems" question is whether or not those systems are executed consistently, cohesively, and effectively. Tracking safety actions, resolutions, and process improvement is key to executive oversight.

- **Leadership communication style.** A leader's questioning style strongly influences what others perceive to be important. It also shapes the information flow back to the leader. Adopting a style that concentrates on inputs rather than outputs is vital. Asking not "What are the results?" but rather "How are we thinking about the issues and improvement opportunities?" garners very different kinds of engagement.

NOTES

PREVENTING SERIOUS INJURIES & FATALITIES:

TRANSFORMING OLD PARADIGMS INTO NEW ONES

by Thomas R. Krause, Ph.D.

PREVENTING SERIOUS INJURIES & FATALITIES:

TRANSFORMING OLD PARADIGMS INTO NEW ONES

Up to now, we have described the Zero Index model as a framework for a comprehensive change strategy. The approach has been in the service of clarity; the Zero Index model provides a foundation that helps organizations capture and understand their safety performance in comprehensive terms. Without this broad understanding, it is easy to fall into the difficulties described in the first chapter of this book: changes driven by necessity, and absent an underlying sense of context, often create incomplete, imbalanced, or overly narrow solutions. Without context, organizations often find themselves in a cycle of addressing one pressing need, only having to go back at a later time when another neglected necessity arises.

At the same time we sometimes see specific areas of safety functioning in which a widely accepted paradigm is no longer serving us well. Such is the case with serious injuries and fatalities (SIFs).

In this chapter we look at the work some organizations are now doing to address an old and flawed paradigm, using what is still useful but adding needed innovation to improve effectiveness in what is perhaps the most important work organizational leaders take on in safety: the problem of serious and fatal injury prevention.

THE PROBLEM OF SERIOUS INJURIES AND FATALITIES

Among the things organizational leaders worry about in safety, the occurrence of life-altering injuries tops the list. Certainly, there is concern about preventing the catastrophic event. Leaders in transit organizations worry about having "another Metrolink," mining companies about having a Massey Mine, energy companies about a Three Mile Island. But we find most leaders are also deeply concerned about preventing "smaller" events—the fatal incident that may not make national news or generate bad press, but that devastates a family and community all the same. And life-altering events can't be undone. The damage to life, property, or the environment can take years to repair, if they are reparable at all.

Despite the intense interest in prevention, reductions in serious injury events have significantly lagged the reductions in workplace injuries generally. In the United States, occupational injury rates since 1993 have declined steadily, but during that same period, workplace fatalities have declined at a much slower rate (Figure 10–1). And in some industries and companies the SIF rate has been level or increasing during this time. These results suggest that something important is happening—or not happening. The methods and practices that are effective at reducing low-severity injuries seem to have little effect on the prevention of fatal injuries. And existing constructs and models don't explain why.

Figure 10–1

Fatality and Nonfatality rates, 1993–2010. Source: U.S. Bureau of Labor Statistics.

Serious event prevention, like many safety issues, has been largely shaped by a few concepts that have been accepted as true over the years, but which have never been demonstrated adequately. This "conventional wisdom," called into question by the data on SIFs, has not served safety leaders well. Over the next few pages, we will illustrate how several organizations collaborated to challenge the common assumptions around serious injury and fatality prevention.

AN OLD FRAMEWORK

Serious injury and fatality (SIF) prevention has long had the implicit view that if "smaller" events were reduced, serious ones would be as well (Figure 10-2). This assumption comes from wide acceptance of a major premise of Heinrich's Safety Triangle—a long-standing concept in occupational safety. The Heinrich Safety Triangle (HST) was introduced in H.W. Heinrich's 1931 book, *Industrial Accident Prevention: A Scientific Approach*. At the time, Heinrich was an assistant superintendent of the Engineering and Inspection Division of Travelers Insurance Company. His theory predicts that for every 300 near-miss incidents there will be 29 minor and one major injury. The HST claims two basic relationships, one descriptive and the other predictive:

SIF prevention has long had the implicit view that if "smaller" events were reduced, serious ones would be as well.

1. Frequency and severity are inversely related (Descriptive); and

2. Reductions in minor medical treatment injuries will result in proportionate reductions in more serious injuries (Predictive).

If Heinrich's theory is correct, a consistent decline in total injuries will be accompanied by a decline in SIFs. This idea assumes that most injuries share common root causes, and that less severe injuries have equal potential to be serious. Therefore preventing less severe injuries will also prevent serious injuries and fatalities.

As recordable injuries continued their steady year-on-year decline, and the proportionate reduction in SIFs failed to materialize, many safety leaders began to ask questions about the Heinrich model.

How a Model Unfolds

It would be a serious mistake to disregard the fact that frequent low-severity events indicate the potential for high-severity events. An environment that frequently generates low-severity events harbors systems and cultural and leadership issues that can (and eventually will) generate high-severity events as well. So how is it that the safety triangle could fail to predict the trend we're seeing?

Figure 10-2. The Old Paradigm.

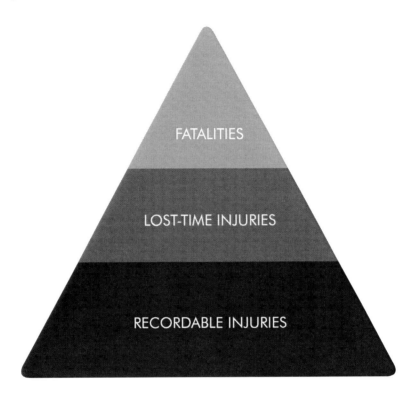

The answer lies in the assumption of a constant ratio between types of injuries. Injuries result from exposure to hazards. But not all exposures are equal in terms of their potential for high-severity events. Some exposures are likely to result in more serious incidents; some in less serious ones. The assumption that all exposures have the same potential for injury (which is essentially what the safety triangle asserts) has affected the day-to-day execution of safety initiatives, leading to several problems:

- **A lack of focus on injuries and near misses that have the potential to result in SIF events.** Failing to distinguish the potential for serious injury across types of injuries leads many organizations to treat all less severe injuries and near misses equally, meaning that an exposure with a low-severity potential gets the same attention as an exposure with a high-severity potential.

- **An increased focus on trivial occurrences.** As organizations fail to realize improvement in severity, many take the inverse relationship a step further and apply a "more is more" approach. That is, they try to improve safety by focusing even more on all exposures, in some cases becoming preoccupied with trivial events.

- **The creative classification of injuries.** Thinking of injuries after the fact as the main area to focus on can lead organizations to categorize injuries creatively.

- **Loss of credibility.** Over-attachment to the safety triangle paradigm, rather than assessing and responding to the exposure picture as it is, can widen the gulf between an organization's management and its employees. In the extreme, this situation can lead to cynicism as employees perceive that safety efforts do not match reality.

- **A general lack of understanding regarding the prevention of SIF events.** Most troubling, of course, is that relying on an overly simplistic view of injury causation limits the ability of an organization to distinguish those exposures that represent the greatest threat to employee life.

Clearly, there are flaws with the existing paradigm of serious and fatal injury prevention. Rather than simply adopting new assumptions, however, it is critical to examine existing ideas against the data.

TAKING A FRESH LOOK

In 2010, seven global companies, ExxonMobil, PotashCorp, Shell, BHP Billiton, Cargill, Archer Daniels Midland Company, and Maersk, joined a study group supported by Mercer/ORC and BST to better understand the inconsistency between the historic principle of the safety triangle and recent injury and fatality statistics at the national and company level. The objective was to research these questions:

- Is the Heinrich safety triangle valid?

- Can a new paradigm better describe causation for serious injuries and fatalities?

- What are the implications of a paradigm shift for planning and executing injury prevention interventions?

Ultimately, the study sought to inform a new model for serious event prevention. Initial results of this study were released in 2011[1]. The findings have helped shed light on SIF causation—and have challenged some of safety's

1   A full report of the study, findings, and methods is available at www.bstsolutions.com

core assumptions. The study showed two primary reasons why fewer less serious injuries don't necessarily create a proportionate reduction in SIFs:

1. The causes and correlates of serious injury and fatality events are *usually different* than those of less serious injuries; and

2. The potential for serious injury is low for the majority (about 80%) of non-SIF injuries.

In other words, *traditional safety efforts often fail to address SIFs because they're not designed to*. There are several immediate implications of this study and its findings for safety leaders:

Understanding SIFs is More Complex Than Previously Thought

While it turns out that Heinrich's safety triangle is accurate descriptively (less severe injuries do occur more frequently than more severe injuries) it is not accurate predictively (there is not a constant ratio between injury types as some people assert). In a similar way, other assumptions about accident causation (that it's either "technical failure" or "human error") or metrics (e.g., that low injury rates indicate that safety generally is well managed), are proving to be over simplified, inaccurate, and—often—downright harmful.

We Have the Data We Need—If We Know Where to Look For It

Serious events are not random as is sometimes assumed. Certain kinds of situations trigger, precede, or cause SIFs—and these precursors are embedded in the way work is done. The problem is, most organizations do not have consistent visibility of this data; precursors are often buried in the data sets of injuries and near misses and their significance is not apparent without a longitudinal (over time) study.

Prevention Initiatives Need to Be Multi-Dimensional

Treating all exposures equally, while well-intended, doesn't make sense when roughly 80% of injuries represent low severity potential. Getting sufficient resources focused on the smaller subset of exposures that present high-severity potential requires systems adaptable to variances in potential.

SIF Prevention Requires a Strategic Approach

Effective SIF prevention ultimately requires that organizations learn to become sensitive to presently hidden data that indicate impending problems. Getting that done is a leadership issue. Leaders must take the initiative to assure that SIF precursors become visible and that resources are allocated to address them.

THE CRITICAL IMPORTANCE OF CAUSES AND CORRELATES

One of the signal findings of the study group is that there are specific precursors associated with serious injury and fatality events. An SIF precursor is a high-risk situation in which management controls are either absent, ineffective, or not complied with, and which will result in a serious or fatal injury if allowed to continue.

SIF precursor data are readily identifiable from longitudinal analysis of available safety data. Most organizations do not have consistent visibility of this data, however, because they do not distinguish injuries with high potential for SIF from those with low potential for SIF. In many organizations, injury data is collected, and action is taken, based on the severity of the injury itself. The new findings on SIF events, however, show us that we can't take actual outcome as an indicator of the exposure present. Consider two separate incidents in which an employee suffers a back strain. On the surface—and in the data—the situations are identical. But when you take a closer look, you notice that:

An SIF precursor is a high-risk situation in which management controls are either absent, ineffective, or not complied with, and which will result in a serious or fatal injury if allowed to continue.

- One worker's injury occurred as he was walking across a parking lot and slipped, wrenching his back in the process.

- The other worker's injury happened when he fell from the top of a rail car. His car was struck by another car being moved into position. The worker fell to the ground and the only injury resulting was a strained back muscle.

If both situations were repeated, we could reasonably expect the worker in the parking lot to see a similar or better outcome. But how likely is it that the worker on top of the rail car would again escape with just a minor injury? In the old safety paradigm, the first instance (the parking lot exposure) would be given attention equal to the second instance (the rail car). Yet, the potential present in each incident could not be more different.

SIFs do not occur randomly, and they are virtually never isolated events; however, the span of SIF precursors is not fully apparent unless incidents are studied longitudinally—a research method involving repeated observations of the same events over long periods of time. This research is rarely applied to the study of work-related injuries. Numerous companies have, however, studied their SIFs and found situation-based and activity-based variables associated with them. These variables are most frequently associated with basic safety system integrity. (Table 10-1).

Table 10-1. Examples of Activities and Situations Likely to Have SIF Precursors

SITUATIONS	ACTIVITIES
• Process instability	• Mobile equipment (operation and interaction with pedestrians)
• Significant process upsets	• Confined space entry
• Unexpected maintenance	• Jobs that require lock out/tag out
• Unexpected changes	• Lifting operations
• High energy potential jobs	• Working at height
• Emergency shutdown procedures	• Process equipment and pipe opening
	• Hot work permits

Examples of SIF precursors identified from the data sets in the study included:

- In order to change the doctor roll on a paper re-roller, two workers must stand beneath it and guide it. The doctor roll weighs about six tons.

- A worker is working on the bottom of an elevated vessel. There is no approved place to secure the lanyard.

- During an emergency shutdown, workers are unable to follow the procedure because it is not understood and appears impractical.

Accounting for the more complex causes and circumstances related to SIF events allows organizations to develop a more focused effort on their prevention. Figure 10–3 illustrates this new paradigm and shows the specific elements that lead to serious events.

Figure 10–3. A New Paradigm for Understanding SIF.

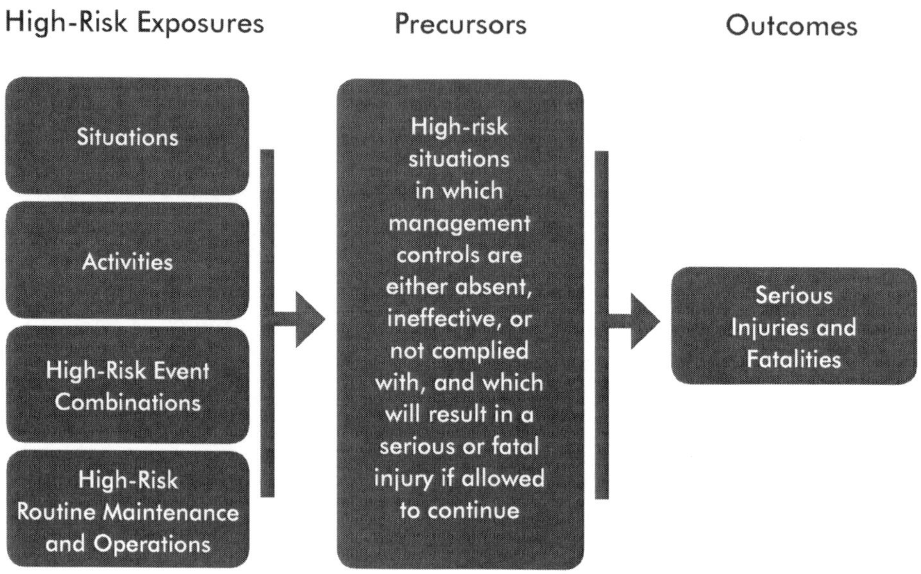

High-Risk Exposures	Precursors	Outcomes
Situations Activities High-Risk Event Combinations High-Risk Routine Maintenance and Operations	High-risk situations in which management controls are either absent, ineffective, or not complied with, and which will result in a serious or fatal injury if allowed to continue	Serious Injuries and Fatalities

A major step in the prevention of SIF events is the identification of SIF precursors. This can be done with longitudinal analysis of injury data, predictive analytics, in-depth analysis of high-risk activities, and observation and interview techniques to discover underlying factors. Often the data needed to accomplish these things is inadequate or missing altogether. New approaches are needed for incident investigation and root cause analysis as well as data systems that capture the relevant data needed to identify SIF precursors.

What old paradigms does your organization hold on to?

BUILDING ON A NEW PARADIGM

Understanding the nature of serious and fatal injuries is not an academic exercise but a practical one. New findings provide a starting point for change in how this critically important aspect of safety is managed. And they illustrate the importance of developing high functioning in all of the Zero Index disciplines. The implications are profound both for the organizations that apply the new principles and for the workers, families, and communities who count on them.

The study group specifically mentions four steps that leaders and their organizations can take to begin addressing SIF events.

1. Educate Key Stakeholders about Serious Injuries and Fatalities.

Thomas Kuhn once observed that people won't let go of an old paradigm—even in the face of overwhelming counter evidence—until there is a new paradigm to replace it. In organizational safety terms, this means that to launch true change, leaders must present a complete picture of what SIF events are and how they are created. People need to be able to see SIFs in their true context. Specifically, we need to show why SIFs are not random events but the culmination of precursors that are both distinct from the causes of less serious events and also detectable. Educating key stakeholders in this new paradigm provides a framework and common vocabulary essential to designing effective interventions.

2. Establish an SIF Rate and Give It Wide Visibility.

Many of the catastrophic events of the last several years (e.g., BP Texas City, Qinghe Special Steel Corp., Upper Big Branch Mine) illustrate the critical role of metrics (the Scorecard discipline) in SIF prevention. In virtually every case the incident was preceded by years in which the rate of recordable injuries was low, very low, or improving. In retrospect, the indicators of impending disaster were potentially available—but they weren't detected with the measures traditionally tracked in safety performance. These missed opportunities reflect confusion and misunderstanding of the relationship between minor and severe injuries, and between personal safety and process safety; and it points to the negative effect of the unexamined safety triangle. Organizations need to establish the frequency with which SIF events and potential events are occurring. This data is critically important because it tells the organization how large the exposure for SIF events is, and allows tracking to determine if improvement efforts are working effectively.

3. Identify the Precursors to SIFs.

An SIF precursor is an unmitigated high-risk situation that has a high probability of resulting in serious injury if repeated. What categorizes a precursor event is not its immediate outcome, but its potential to produce a serious outcome. A variety of techniques are useful in the identification of SIF precursors including predictive analytics, analysis of high-risk activities and discovery by observation and interview. Each organization needs to identify its own unique SIF precursors.

4. Examine Safety Systems to Determine Their Effectiveness at Mitigating Precursors and Integrate the Findings of the Research Described in this Section.

What existing safety systems in your organization address the underlying factors that cause SIF events? Do behavioral observations, audits, incident investigations, pre-task risk assessments, and other systems address SIFs?

WHAT THE FINDINGS MEAN

It is no coincidence that failures in many of the 10 Zero Index disciplines (introduced in chapter 4) so often appear in the investigations of serious and catastrophic events. But persistent patterns of injury events fundamentally start with the Foundational discipline of Exposure (chapter 5). An organization's thinking about injury causation determines its focus in safety. And the more limited the understanding of injury causation, the more limited the range of possible solutions.

At the lower end of the Exposure discipline (see Table 5–3), where injuries are believed to be uncontrollable (Chaotic stage) or the fault of the workers involved (Singular stage), it can be near impossible to enact needed changes in Culture, Leadership, Structure, and so on—simply because the organization's taxonomy of causes doesn't account for them. (One could argue, too, that low functioning in the Scorecard discipline reinforces poor Exposure functioning by failing to provide complete information about injuries and their causes.)

How is the functioning of different Zero Index disciplines manifested in your organization?

This is not to say that leaders of organizations in the lower ranges of Exposure, or any other discipline, are acting in bad faith, or that they cannot develop a more sophisticated understanding (many can and do.) Rather, the point is to acknowledge that our ideas themselves can be limiting. In order to improve, we must first understand why we think what we do and understand what works, and what doesn't, in our existing framework. In our experience, the thinking that hinders progress in the prevention of serious injuries and fatalities comes from many commonly held ideas about injuries—specifically, ideas about the relationship between severity and frequency.

In undertaking a study of SIF events, these seven organizations have shown the value of thinking beyond existing assumptions. Like other innovations, this was only possible by first asking what is possible.

NOTES

NOTES

DEVELOPING A NEW MINDSET FOR SAFETY

by Colin Duncan

DEVELOPING A NEW MINDSET FOR SAFETY

West Carrollton is your typical small town in middle America, where high school football reigns king every Friday night in the fall. Its 13,818 residents live seven miles south of Dayton, Ohio, close to the Indiana border. Minutes after midnight on May 4, 2009, highly flammable vapor was released from a hazardous waste recycling operation occupying about 20 acres in West Carrollton. The vapor ignited and exploded. One employee suffered first-degree burns and a second employee broke his pelvis when pinned by a row of crashing personnel lockers. Two others suffered minor injuries running to escape the fireballs. About 72 employees work the day shift at the site; just six were on the clock the night of May 4.

A sequence of blasts damaged every structure on the site to the extent the U.S. Chemical Safety Board was unable to collect enough evidence to reach concrete root cause conclusions. Nearby homes and businesses were rocked, with residents reporting broken windows, bent garage doors, and detached chimneys. Five neighboring offices suffered buckling masonry walls and broken ceilings, suggesting workers might have been injured had they been present at the time of the explosion. The U.S. Chemical Safety Board's reported preliminary cost estimates, including lost production, property damage, and business disruption, totaled about $27 million. Surveillance cameras recorded fireballs continuing to explode for about 45 minutes after the initial blast. By 10:38 in the morning of May 4, the fire was declared under control.

How closely do safety activities match your actual risk profile?

The West Carrollton event made headlines in the local press but was little noticed outside the Dayton area. Most would consider an event like this too small to matter to leaders outside this particular company or this particular industry. But consider this: the company that owned and ran the facility was a credible operator. It was a member of the Environmental Technology Council, a national trade association of commercial, environmental firms that recycle, treat, and dispose of industrial and hazardous waste. The business was a publicly-traded subsidiary of a global environmental corporation with more than 300,000 employees. Three of the company's sites had qualified as "Star" facilities in OSHA's Voluntary Protection Program. The West Carrollton site itself was inspected by the Ohio EPA two times a year and audited by customers between 30 and 40 times a year.

In other words, the West Carrollton event embodies the problem that faces leaders in every industry, in every country, every day—that you can "do all the right things" and still not assure the safety of your employees, and of those who interact with your operations and products. Solving this problem is the fundamental charge of the safety leader. As leaders face ever greater

You can "do all the right things" and still not assure the safety of your employees, and of those who interact with your operations and products.

challenges in technical complexity, increased legal accountability, a shortage of qualified safety expertise, and other issues, relying on old ideas about risk, and how to manage and mitigate it, is no longer sufficient.

The Zero Index disciplines provide the tools for establishing organizational functioning that effectively and systematically reduces risk. However, it requires executive leaders to set the process in motion. As leaders, we must first develop the ability ourselves to understand and respond accurately to risk in the organization. What we understand—what we know—becomes what we act upon.

LEARNING FROM THE PAST

What happened in West Carrollton and what can leaders learn from it? The Chemical Safety Board was unable to determine the precise cause of the overpressure event due to widespread damage to the process area. What we do know is that immediately prior to the release that led to the explosion, the unit operator had started the shutdown of a tetrahydrofuran (THF) solvent recovery process in a so-called dirty tank after test results indicated that the material had reached the threshold preventing further distillation. The Chemical Safety Board concluded that uncontrolled venting, either through the vacuum breaker or a mismanifolded line, allowed vapors to accumulate to explosive concentrations outside process equipment.[1]

The West Carrollton site operated under multiple layers of control systems. In addition to state EPA inspections and scores of customer audits, the processing operation followed codes and standards of the National Fire Protection Association, the Center for Chemical Process Safety, and OSHA's process safety management standard.

Still, in a post-incident inspection, OSHA cited the facility for numerous violations of the PSM standard, alleging the company failed to conduct compliance audits every three years. OSHA also found worker training deficien-

---

1   www.csb.gov/assets/document/Veolia_Case_Study.pdf

cies, inadequate testing and inspections of piping and processes, and lack of written standards for operating procedures and maintaining mechanical integrity of equipment.

As leaders, the West Carrollton example (like many before it) offers two critical lessons:

First, this event shows us that layers of protocols and precautions from federal agencies and voluntary organizations cannot eliminate the risk of a potentially devastating incident. The small operation had multiple checks and balances that ought to have provided assurances, both to its operating executives and to industry, that the plant was operating safely. These control systems failed.

The second thing we should appreciate is that a razor-thin margin exists between an after-midnight incident involving a skeleton crew that makes the front page of a local newspaper, and a catastrophe that makes the national news. If the release had occurred at seven minutes past noon instead of midnight, more than seven times the number of employees would have been on site: 77 versus 6. The lab/operations building that housed the source of the ignition—where three concrete walls buckled out and roof panels blew apart—would have been occupied by non-essential personnel on the day shift. The surrounding homes and small businesses would not have been dark and settled in for the night; residents and customers would have been out and about on the streets. Instead of a midnight incident that injured four employees, two seriously, West Carrollton could have been a major event with possibly multiple fatalities involving workers and citizens.

THE LEADER'S CHALLENGE—SEEING AND UNDERSTANDING RISK

Most senior leaders work in corporate environments that look and feel very different from sites they own and operate, such as older operations, congested and confined by tanks, pumps, and other equipment, that composed the layout in West Carrollton.

The operator of the West Carrollton facility is based in Chicago. The company operates 72 collection facilities and 29 solid waste sanitary landfills in 12 states, the Bahamas, and Canada. In this type of

Most senior leaders work in corporate environments that look and feel very different from sites they own and operate.

complex business, at what level are leaders made aware of potential multi-million-dollar risks such as those identified by the Chemical Safety Board in West Carrollton? Who was aware that vent devices were inadequately designed to control or contain hazardous and/or toxic vapor; or that the lab/operations building, which housed the source of the ignition, was not classified under the National Electrical Code NFPA 70? Who was aware that no record existed of a process hazard analysis to evaluate the siting of the lab/operations building so close to the operating units?

West Carrollton is only one example. Consider whether you as a senior leader have absolute confidence that your organization has in place the systems necessary to prevent the kinds of tragedies that rocked industry globally in 2010-2011?

- The Tesoro refinery explosion in Anacortes, Washington, April 2, 2010, killed five workers.

- The Massey Energy Upper Big Branch mine explosion April 5, 2010, in West Virginia resulted in 29 miner deaths.

- Eleven workers died in the BP Deepwater Horizon explosion in the Gulf of Mexico April 20, 2010.

- Four employees were fatally injured in the PG&E pipeline explosion in San Bruno, California, September 9, 2010.

- The two-month entrapment of 33 Chilean miners in 2010.

- The March, 2011, disaster at Japan's Fukushima Daiichi nuclear plant, when an earthquake and tsunami knocked out cooling systems, releasing radiation as reactors suffered meltdown.

What information would you need to prevent similar events in your own organization? How sure are you that, right now, you would get that information? As safety leaders, we must constantly strive to ask questions about our systems, disciplines, and procedures. Successful safety leadership is about a constant drive to uncover unrealized or unassessed risk and to seek to create visibility of this risk at all levels in the organization.

Safety's Information Problem

Recently, when working with a group of senior leaders, we set out a blank sheet of paper and asked them to describe the kind of data they'd need to ensure consistent safety improvement year after year. What would that data look like? How would they find it? The leaders mulled over the metrics they were used to: OSHA recordable rates, total case rates, lost workdays, and similar regulatory figures. Ultimately, the sheet remained blank.

Why was that? As the leaders themselves recognized, the problem wasn't motivation. Like other executives, these leaders genuinely cared about the wellbeing of their people. They were also highly accomplished in other areas. So why would they struggle so much with safety?

A large part of the answer lies with traditional safety thinking. Leaders have been trained to ask questions about lagging indicators. In many operations, "safety leadership" is more accurately described as management by exception—leaders respond to events, rather than anticipate and remove risks.

In our experience, there is often considerable disconnect between operational safety disciplines and systems integrity and how senior executives understand these disciplines. Simply put, many leaders have insufficient knowledge and understanding of operating risk about safety to ask the right questions. This is entirely appropriate in one sense. We want safety managed at the lowest appropriate level of the organization. We want people closest to the risks to know them best. At the same time, the information flowing back up from the lowest level, the feedback loop, is often incomplete. The result is that leaders lack the ability to act (not knowing there is a risk) or they act on the wrong things (having poor or incomplete information).

The challenge for senior leaders is learning how to deepen their understanding of risk such that they can effectively support safety systems and the people they rely on to execute them.

Often the only safety metrics that receive good visibility at senior levels are the OSHA recordable rates mentioned previously. The advantage of this data is that they give senior leaders a convenient way to compare safety performance one year to the next, from one division or operating unit to the next, to benchmark these outcomes against peer competitors in their particular industry.

But there is a downside. OSHA data and similar lagging and regulatory metrics are one-dimensional. They focus only on people and events, what happened or didn't happen, according to the numbers. The data can lead senior executives to believe they have an understanding of risk, not appreciating that understanding is based solely on personal safety and that it represents only part of the picture. Leadership is left with a less-than holistic appraisal of safety risks across the entire operation. Process safety is overshadowed by the attention focused on personal safety rates. Sadly, this focus often leads to senior leaders celebrating success, through awards and other recognition, and in doing so undermining credibility and reinforcing an erroneous message about what is important. What we find is often missing from the metrics (and therefore the focus) are things like the mechanical

Bias starts with OSHA expectations about what gets reported, it is compounded by safety executives focusing on these data, and it is locked in because operational leaders learn to ask only about this data.

integrity of equipment, repair orders left open, and the adequacy of testing and inspecting processes.

We should be clear that this bias in reporting is a function of several dynamics. It starts with OSHA expectations about what gets reported, it is compounded by safety executives focusing on these data, and it is locked in because operational leaders learn to ask only about this data. Senior leadership is often left not knowing what questions to ask to ascertain the true nature of risk in their operations, or the associated level of safety that falls under leadership's governance.

In our work, we see that this lack of a framework for capturing risk information is problematic in several ways:

- Few companies compile and review records of near-miss incidents.

- Process safety management performance measures are often inaccessible to safety personnel (never mind senior executives)—being "owned" by engineering or operations departments. So to senior leaders, safety appears to be about people, not systems.

- The Responsible CARE program initiated by the chemical industry after the Bhopal catastrophe did a good job gathering process safety management data. OSHA's PSM standard does a good job. But too often PSM is not integrated with personal data due to organizational silos, departments, and dispersed owners.

- The lack of a holistic scorecard of safety performance metrics leads to a fixation on singular "one-off" events causing injury. Systemic root causes are missed, the worker gets the blame, and the solution is more training.

- Workers operate under supervision and within systems and organizational cultures that value safety to varying degrees. Many leaders do not possess data on employer and supervisor perceptions of cultural safety values—the ground level view of "the way things are done around here."

These problems surfaced recently in a research project we conducted with a group of large organizations. We asked for data that represented their exposure to risk. Each organization provided us with the same data they report to external parties, such as OSHA, the Bureau of Labor Statistics, or peer-group safety councils for benchmarking. Despite the volume of information, none of it included any metrics relating to process safety management. This is a common challenge when looking at safety performance and one that can be readily addressed through rigorous attention to reporting disciplines and process.

FEEDING LEADERSHIP CURIOSITY

Most leaders are naturally inquisitive. They want to know how things work and how to make systems and teams more effective. Leaders are no different in safety. Many leaders we know are deeply curious about risk reduction efforts and routinely ask questions about them. *Are our processes working as they should? Where are the risks to life-altering injuries? Are we spending our resources the right way?* The better-informed the leader the more effective her curiosity is at driving reduction in organizational risk. The challenge of engaging leaders in safety is not so much generating their interest (many are already deeply interested) it is getting leaders the right information.

What kind of information do your leaders need to drive a reduction in all organizational risks?

How do we build a framework that provides a steady stream of complete risk information? How do we make sure that our leaders review and analyze feedback and data from a host of reporting points? We want to show them more than year-end summaries, which do little to pique their interest or leverage their abilities. We want to show leaders ongoing activities and assessments that capture safety and health performance in real-time. We want to show leaders what they can *do.*

Some companies have demonstrated how to build such frameworks for understanding and responding to risk. For example, ExxonMobil's Operations Integrity Management System requires that:[2]

- Precursors that can lead to incidents be recorded, analyzed, and addressed;

- Actual incidents and significant near-misses be quickly investigated to identify root causes and contributing factors;

---

2   www.exxonmobil.com/Corporate/safety_ops

- Potential consequences determine the level of investigation; and

- Findings lead to interventions necessary to prevent recurrence.

At the other end of industry, Best Buy's incident review system[3] includes:

- Any event that results in injury (customer and employee), whether the injury requires medical treatment or not;

- Any event that results in damage to customer property;

- Emergency situations (fire, flooding, etc.) that result in damage to property, structural damage to a building, or a business interruption; and

- Near miss incidents and accidents that did not involve injury, but had a potential for causing a serious event.

These systems and others like them are still the exceptions. But they point the way toward a new mindset where collecting, analyzing, and acting on risk precursors and exposures is no longer a novelty for the progressive few, but a standard practice for all responsible organizations. Fundamentally, senior leaders need to have at their fingertips the information necessary to understand and ensure that:

- Integrity in all disciplines required for safety is created and executed from the top of the organization downward.

- Expectations of execution of these disciplines are explicit in the operational day-to-day.

- The mindset exists to achieve the optimum level across all 10 Zero Index disciplines. This consists of the Foundational disciplines of Vision, Engagement, and Exposure. The Safety disciplines of Structure, Scorecard, Expertise, and Safety-Enabling Systems. And the Organizational disciplines of Leadership, Culture, and Sustaining Systems. These are described in detail in chapters 4, 5, 6, and 7 of this book.

- The proper governance, management, stewardship, and implementation of safety at every level of the organization. Safety execution at every level is the bar we are setting.

---

3   www.bestbuy.com

A CALL TO ACTION

The intent of what you have read in the previous pages of this book is to create a new paradigm for how executives and leaders in different roles think about, communicate, execute, and monitor safety-related expectations, responsibilities, and engagement.

What are your action items for leading a zero-harm organization?

The following is intended to be a list of actionable items for leaders. Management credibility is essential to employee engagement. When we ask for discretionary efforts from employees on behalf of safety our actions must speak for us, not our words. These actions are far more powerful than any communication strategy we can devise. As we all know, our staff judge us by what we do, not what we say.

Senior Executive Action Items

- Have or create a model (or framework) that you can use to explain to the organization all of the constituent parts of safety. Be able to answer the question, "What goes into running a world-class safety organization?" Demonstrate to employees at all levels that operational executives understand the meaning and significance of these constituents.

- Invest sufficient time to understand the body of major safety disciplines in operations, including the key technical and management systems for preventing catastrophic events: process safety information, process hazard assessment, operating procedures, training, contractor management, mechanical integrity, non-routine work authorization, management of change, incident investigation, emergency planning and response, and self-audits. Sufficient knowledge of essentials such as human factors, culture, behavior, and safety leadership, is also a necessity.

- Leaders should also understand, and be able to converse in, some core safety concepts such as the hierarchy of controls, James Reason's lines of defense, and root cause analysis, just to name a few.

- Focus on the big rocks: look at those things that create risk exposure to events that threaten lives or the viability of the operation. While unlikely or infrequent, make sure you're paying attention to events that could lead to significant loss of life, environmental damage, or property loss.

- Understand data differently. Stop asking about recordable rates and start asking about critical data that take into account potential upstream systemic incident causal factors including management behaviors and decisions, risk assessment, facility design and construction, maintenance, management of change, management of contractors, and requirements for incident investigation, analysis, and corrective action.

- Have a strategy. Be able to articulate safety expectations and performance levels five years down the road. Of course this includes goals and objectives. But critical here is to focus on the important inputs that contribute to strategy—employee feedback, observations, reporting of near misses and incidents, investigative findings, audit findings—rather than on delivering outputs such as OSHA recordables.

- Focus on governance. Create a safety governance structure that is world class. Describe how senior safety leadership flows into operational leadership and how that flows into employee engagement.

- As an executive leader, identify the three behaviors you must continuously demonstrate to support your safety strategy effectively. But also identify the three behaviors you need to work on (i.e. change) in order to make the strategy work and show renewed leadership. This is a relatively simple task but one that can have huge leverage. By clearly understanding and demonstrating what you will stop, start, or continue doing and how that drives your safety strategy, you send a powerful and easily interpreted message to those around you. This is a pragmatic exercise. There is no need to try to follow a 20-item checklist. Focus rather on a small set of high-gain actions and behaviors.

- Scrutinize and understand the safety decision-making process in your organization. Don't just ask retrospectively why people made a decision. Focus on understanding decisions and actions as they are happening.

These same eight action items can and should be calibrated for site management and operational leaders and safety executives.

Site Management and Operational Leaders Action Items

- As part of communicating to the organization all of the constituent parts of safety, you must pay close attention to how people are recognized, rewarded, and promoted for safety. Be clear on expectations. Ensure safety is considered in contractor selection. Determine the number of needed safety professionals, and their roles. Determine the rigor of the safety orientation of new hires. Determine how an operation manager's previous safety track record enters into promotion considerations.

- Invest time in understanding safety-enabling systems and safety-sustaining systems. Ask what systems are now in place. What is the basis for choosing those you have? Are they selected based on regulatory compliance alone or risk assessment? Ask what systems you have in place to address exposures that have a high potential for causing life-altering injuries.

- Ensure risk-based safety-enabling systems are used by employees, supervisors, managers, and contractors alike to identify and mitigate risks. Ensure risk-based policies, procedures, and rules are applied consistently. Your goal is to anticipate and prepare for future risks.

- Stop asking about recordable rates and start asking about critical data that take into account potential upstream systemic incident causal factors. Recognize safety outcomes are most often driven by a steady succession of organizational decisions and actions that shape the day-to-day execution of safety objectives.

- Your strategy should be shaped by the goals you set for safety, the cultural value you place on people (commodities versus assets), how you view injury causation (including upstream root causes), the role and funding of safety professionals, the scorecard you use to monitor and measure safety performance, and the adherence you insist on to process safety and the discipline required every minute, every day to achieve your goals.

- Educate yourself on the principles of effective safety leadership. Be open to challenging your assumptions. Consider how you communicate about safety. When talking about production, is the conversation about safe production? Do you talk about serious injuries and fatalities in terms of numbers, or by names of people? And ask yourself: Would you want your son or daughter to work in one of your facilities in an entry-level job?

- Give honest and complete feedback about safety, especially when the message is unfavorable. On the plus side, perhaps you need to continue your efforts to seek out feedback and coaching on your safety performance.

- Stay close to day-to-day safety decision making. Decisions influence an organization's safety culture. That culture is critical to your success as a site manager or operational leader. Decisions include hiring and training for safety positions; implementing processes for defining individual safety performance expectations and tracking performance; deciding how much time you are going to spend out on the floor regularly observing and reviewing the degree of employee engagement in safety. Decisions such as these will influence the extent to which safety is integrated with the business.

Safety Executive Action Items

- Create a formal framework that supports safety decision-making, accountability, and action. A robust governance structure provides rigor and constancy.

- Ensure safety roles and responsibilities are defined at all levels throughout the organization. Further, ensure people have the skills, competence, knowledge, processes, and procedures to identify and report on exposures across all of these roles and levels.

- Use a scorecard that extends beyond the traditional incident metrics. Pay attention to ensuring your organization's metrics reveal a clear picture of risk and don't inadvertently oversimplify or mask the true picture.

- Ensure your strategy, goal setting, and oversight are supported by senior executive leaders.

- Safety leaders must adopt the role of advisor and facilitator to executive management, board members, and senior operations leaders to sponsor safety improvement in a collaborative manner. This collaboration requires leadership from the top, with safety professionals shifting from technical experts and auditors to counsel and coach.

- Again, focus on the critical behaviors of greatest leverage to achieving the strategy. For example, perhaps you need to move from an injury-focus to an exposure-reduction focus. You might take too much ownership of the safety role and not delegate enough. You might be too much of an enforcer, not enough of a coach and facilitator. To the positive, perhaps you need to continue to ensure that behavior-based safety does not descend into a mind-numbing, box-checking, exercise. Continue your championing of leading indicators of safety performance.

THE ZERO INDEX ORGANIZATION

This is the way the Zero Index disciplines model becomes integrated into the values, beliefs, and actions that create a Zero Index organization:

- Create a new mental model for safety.

- Understand and master the requisite disciplines.

- Pay attention to low-frequency/high-consequence events and near-misses.

- Think differently about safety-related data. Don't allow the organization to become complacent due to low rates of low-severity injuries. The causes and correlates of serious injuries are usually different than those of less serious injuries.

- Set high benchmarks for thorough, quality incident investigations. Do not merely identify technical causes and "operator error." Track down and correct those upstream causes. Do not settle for superficial findings.

- Articulate your strategic objectives and timelines for safety performance. Employee input into strategy formulation is key—for their frontline knowledge and experience is unique.

- Be firm on governance. Your governance structure should be a roadmap for employees at all levels to apply on the job regularly. Enlist all levels of the organization to make governance relevant, a regular part of business conversations and staff meetings. Be alert to disconnects that might arise with new hires, employees in new positions, contractors, temporary help, newly acquired businesses, employees working and traveling on their own, and operations in different cultures around the globe.

- Keep it simple and focus on crucial behaviors you are already doing that support safety. Think how to leverage those to the maximum. Identify through feedback a certain few behaviors you need to change, or adopt, to support safety.

- Stay on top of safety decisions and activities. Be proactive and anticipatory in recognizing and mitigating precursors and exposures to potential harm. Don't be outcome-based, waiting for injury reports to land on your desk.

As I mentioned in the introduction, our objective in writing this book is to help you to think and act in ways that help you both assess your current stage of safety functioning effectively and efficiently and also determine your interventions for improvements. It is important to avoid quick fixes, fads, and misleading measurements as you close the gap between where you are and where you want to be—to have integrity and confidence in your comprehensive, all-encompassing, world class safety functions and performance.

Safety improvement is not about programs, initiatives, or projects. It's about systemic, methodical disciplined management, oversight, execution, and sustained focus.

We wish you well in your pursuit of Zero.

NOTES

NOTES

ABOUT THE AUTHORS

Colin Duncan is BST's chief executive officer. He drives the strategy, vision, and innovation to ensure delivery of sustainable safety improvements across complex global operations and cultures.

A widely sought-after speaker, Colin presents at conferences and seminars around the world, discussing strategies for sustainable performance improvement, safety deployment, and the impact of different cultures on safety.

Originally from the U.K., Colin earned a bachelor's degree from King's College London. He now lives in Massachusetts.

Don Groover is a senior vice president at BST, working across all types of industries to help organizations create high-performing safety cultures and systems.

He has contributed to a number of books, including "Leading with Safety," by BST founder Tom Krause, and has also authored and co-authored numerous articles that have appeared in a variety of industry publications.

Don holds master's degrees in education and environmental health sciences.

Guy Boyd is the regional general manager for BST across Europe, Middle East, and Africa, overseeing all business development, intervention design, operations, and client service delivery for the region.

With a wealth of multi-cultural and international expertise in management consulting, Guy is an experienced executive consultant and coach, and is a regular international conference presenter.

Guy holds a bachelor's degree in business studies from the University of Bradford, and lives in the U.K.

Jim Huggett is a senior vice president at BST, where he has coached more than 200 senior and enterprise-level executives, and led successful organizational culture change initiatives around the country.

He is an effective and frequent public speaker, and his award-winning work on organizational development and culture has been published in the national business press.

Jim earned his master's degree in business management from Webster University in Missouri.

As a senior vice president for BST, **Jim Spigener** advises corporate leaders around the globe on how to leverage their roles to dramatically improve safety performance. He has helped companies worldwide to design, prepare, and implement successful safety solutions at every organizational level, from senior leaders to shop floor personnel.

A highly regarded speaker, Jim has also co-authored books, as well as articles that have been published in a variety of industry and trade journals. He lives in Texas.

As a vice president at BST, **Kristen Bell** designs and leads strategic initiatives that reduce fatalities and injuries, strengthen safety culture, and improve overall organizational effectiveness.

Partnering with senior leadership teams and other key stakeholders, Kristen brings custom-fit solutions that produce measurable results in challenging and complex situations.

Kristen earned a master's degree in clinical psychology from California State University-Northridge, and an MBA from California Lutheran University.

Richard Russell is managing director and co-founder of Russell Consulting, BST's affiliate in Australia, New Zealand, and Papua New Guinea.

A specialist in occupational medicine for more than 25 years, he also has 18 years of experience leading development and integration of safety, health, and environmental strategy and services in the industrial arena.

His education includes bachelor's degrees in medicine and surgery from the University of Adelaide, and a master's degree in public health from Sydney University.

Ricky Yu is BST's regional general manager in Asia, responsible for guiding BST growth, as well as the implementation of technical development and consulting services, in the area. He has over 22 years of experience in environmental health and safety management and operations.

Ricky holds several degrees, including a master's degree in international and public affairs from the University of Hong Kong, and an executive MBA from the University of Western Ontario in Canada. He lives in Singapore.

As an executive vice president for BST, **Sarah Smith** oversees client partnerships and implementations in the chemicals, water utilities, metals and mining, and rail industries.

A dynamic consultant, Sarah specializes in helping organizations adapt improvement strategies such as multi-rater feedback and developmental planning.

Sarah has a master's degree in communications and management from Texas Tech University, and a bachelor's degree in communications from Midwestern State University.

As president at BST, **Scott Stricoff** oversees the company's consulting work and personally assists clients in improving safety leadership, management, and culture.

Scott works with multi-national clients to provide safety and health management system assessments and audits. His work informs compliance verification for boards of directors, pre-acquisition risk assessment, and overall performance evaluation.

Scott earned an MBA from Northeastern University and a bachelor's degree in chemical engineering from MIT.

A leader in human-performance technology, **Ted Apking** helps executives understand and apply the principles of behavioral science to successfully implement critical strategic safety initiatives.

As an executive vice president, Ted has global responsibility for BST's extensive work in the oil and gas industry. He specializes in improving engineering, procurement, and contractor safety performance in energy development projects.

Ted lives in the Michigan area, and holds a doctorate in applied behavior analysis from Western Michigan University.

Tom Krause is founder and senior advisor on research and thought leadership of BST. Since 1980, Dr. Krause has conducted research and designed interventions for accident and injury prevention, patient safety, quality improvement, culture change, and other targeted applications.

Dr. Krause has authored four books on safety performance improvement, culture change, and leadership. He is presently writing the 2nd edition of "Leading with Safety," a groundbreaking work on safety leadership and culture.

A longtime resident of California, he earned his doctorate at the University of California, Irvine.

INDEX